HOT FLASH DECISIONS

by

Shirley B. Garrett

Positive Directions LLC
Huntsville, Alabama

This is a work of fiction. All of the characters, organizations, and events portrayed in this novel are either products of the author's imagination or are used fictitiously.

HOT FLASH DECISIONS

Copyright © 2020 by Shirley B. Garrett, Psy.D

All rights reserved. No part of this publication may be reproduced, stored in a retrieval system, or transmitted in any form or by any means, electronic, mechanical, photocopying, recording or otherwise, without the written permission of the publisher.

ISBN: 978-1-943065-08-0

Published by Positive Directions LLC, Huntsville, AL.

Cover design by Dan Thompson. Cover photograph by the author.

PREVIOUS BOOKS IN THE HOT FLASH DIVAS SERIES

Hot Flash Divas

Hot Flash Desires

Also by Shirley B. Garrett,

Charlie Stone Crime Thriller Series

Brianna Kelly Paranormal Mystery Series

DEDICATION

This book is dedicated to all the readers who love the Hot Flash Divas.

ACKNOWLEDGMENTS

Writing and publishing a book is an arduous and tedious act of love.

The following people contributed to this process and the book is better because of their efforts.

The Huntsville Literary Association critic group and the Coffee and Critique writer's group offered much advice and support.

My editor, Lisa Prince, once again succeeded in her efforts to keep me on the straight and narrow. Thanks.

My family, friends, and especially my husband, Bob, have been a great support.

All of you make it possible for me to create. Thank you.

Table of Contents

CHAPTER 1: Holiday Madness — 1
CHAPTER 2: Brent — 6
CHAPTER 3: Mike — 11
CHAPTER 4: The Journey Begins — 16
CHAPTER 5: The Race — 23
CHAPTER 6: Peru or Bust — 29
CHAPTER 7: Peru at Last — 31
CHAPTER 8: The First Tour — 42
CHAPTER 9: Shake and Rattle — 48
CHAPTER 10: The Text — 56
CHAPTER 11: The Discussion — 62
CHAPTER 12: Machu Picchu — 67
CHAPTER 13: The Big Surprise — 77
CHAPTER 14: What Happened? — 79
CHAPTER 15: The Big Talk — 83
CHAPTER 16: What Now — 89
CHAPTER 17: Bad News — 98

Table of Contents, continued

CHAPTER 18: Stressed	106
CHAPTER 19: Pandemic!	111
CHAPTER 20: Almost Home	118
CHAPTER 21: The Quarantine Begins	121
CHAPTER 22: A Surprise Visit	124
CHAPTER 23: Paper Crisis	130
CHAPTER 24: Stuck	133
CHAPTER 25: Food Heaven	135
CHAPTER 26: Day Two of Quarantine	141
CHAPTER 27: Mike	146
CHAPTER 28: Day Three	151
CHAPTER 29: The Take Over	154
CHAPTER 30: Delicious Aromas	158
CHAPTER 31: What to Do?	161
CHAPTER 32: The Big Freeze	164
CHAPTER 33: Melting Ice	167
CHAPTER 34: New Revelations	169
CHAPTER 35: Rachael	173
CHAPTER 36: More Information	177
CHAPTER 37: What Now?	180
CHAPTER 38: Home Alone	184
CHAPTER 39: One Last Attempt	191

Table of Contents, continued

CHAPTER 40: Preparing for the Worst   195

CHAPTER 41: Happy Birthday!   198

CHAPTER 42: Sheltering at Home   205

CHAPTER 1: Holiday Madness

Anytime a man is involved, or in my case two, there are problems. I had a situation and needed advice. I pondered how to broach the subject while I sat in my favorite recliner, sipping a beverage that I'd named "A Bit of Jingle." My three BFF's, the Divas, perched on their favorite roosts in my living room while admiring my Peacock-themed Christmas tree.

Latishia Snide, the buxom fashion maven of our foursome, had shed her three-inch, spike-heeled, black ankle boots. She tucked her socked feet under her cranberry sweater dress while relaxing on my love seat. Her long braids were intertwined with narrow red and green ribbons to honor the season.

Buffy, my blonde cocker spaniel, snoozed beside her. She looked up when Latishia spoke.

"I can taste the cranberry juice, but what're the rest of the ingredients?" Latishia asked, smacking her lips.

"White wine, cranberry juice, and Vernor's Ginger Ale," I said as I admired the white tree lights' sparkle through the tinted concoction. "It may have an official name somewhere. I can't believe some bartender hasn't already discovered it."

"So true," Gina Bongiorno said while sweeping abundant dark curls over one shoulder. "Nonna would say this is a bevanda deliziosa."

I peered at Gina, then shook my head with dismay. It seemed incongruent that my friend since parochial school, a successful divorce attorney, had morphed into a Christmas elf the first day of December. She sat curled on one end of my couch wearing a tacky Christmas sweater, Grinch socks, and a Santa hat. I wasn't sure what happened to her psyche this year. Perhaps she was trying to keep her cheer up after losing both of her cats the day after Thanksgiving. Jasmine and Oscar had dashed into the street during a sofa delivery and had been hit by a speeding vehicle.

On the other end of the sofa, petite Kat Wang pulled up the footrest and snuggled into position, before picking up her drink and taking a sip. "I like it." She tucked one side of her blue-black pageboy behind an ear. "I'm a sucker for anything with ginger ale."

I decided to dive into the topic that had been bothering me. "I know the Christmas season is stressful, but having two guys in my life is making it doubly intense this year."

Latishia shook her head in disapproval. "Phoenix Dixie O'Leary —"

Gina interrupted. "Uh, oh. She used your full name. You're in for it now."

Latishia shot Gina a glare. "As I was saying before I was so rudely interrupted, you have two handsome, hot, and successful men at your beck and call. How can that be stressful? If you want to experience stress, come spend a day at the bank. Girl, my customers are harassing me at all hours about their building loans. Some old fool called my cell phone at eleven last night. I didn't think men that age were even awake that late." She flipped a hand in the air. "The world doesn't end if a building loan doesn't clear before Christmas." She reached over and stroked Buffy. "To make matters worse, Dante adds another item to his Christmas list daily. That little man acts like I'm a walking money machine."

"At least things are going well with Aaron," I said, feeling defensive.

She harrumphed. "That man is pushing to get married this spring. Heck, we only got engaged a month ago. I love the man, but I'm feeling rushed. This is a life-long decision."

Gina chuckled and winked. "If marriage was a life-long decision, I wouldn't have a career."

Latishia glared at her over the top of her drink. "I can't believe a good Italian Catholic girl like you would say such a thing."

"Are you forgetting I'm the black sheep of my family? Even Father Joseph lectures me at every opportunity, because I'm not married to a 'good Catholic man.' He believes every married woman in the parish should go forth and procreate a new member for the flock on a yearly basis."

Kat set her glass on the end table and shook her head. "Thank goodness I'm a Buddhist. They don't care if I procreate or not. I think working in the E.R. has you both beat when it comes to stress. Car accidents, knifings, gunshot wounds, overdoses, and a flu outbreak made me crazy when I worked there last year. I'm so glad I went to work for Dr. Howard. Fewer bucks, but also less stress." She lifted her drink to Latishia. "Sister, I can relate to your woes. Jack isn't asking for much this year—only a motorcycle! Like I'm letting my only child have a motorcycle. I'm a nurse! I see what happens to people who ride those cursed machines." She pushed her glasses back in place. "Jack is relentless. He cut out a photo of the one he wants, and Xeroxed it a million times. I keep finding copies of that monster machine everywhere." She leaned forward. "Would you believe the little rascal put a copy in my favorite tea mug this morning?"

Latishia took a sip. "Oh, I believe it. We could swap stories for hours about our two sons. How are things going with Don?"

Kat's foot began to bounce. "Jack loves him. The two have really bonded." The foot bop increased. "My parents are still pushing for a nice Chinese doctor for a son-in-law, not a retired New York cop who's bartending in Fort Walton Beach."

"I'm convinced Jack will win them over in the end," I said.

After a noticeable lag in the conversation, we all turned to look at Gina, who was usually the first to complain.

"Things are fine on my end." Gina said. "My world will turn upside down after January first. No decent person asks for a divorce before Christmas."

Latishia crinkled her nose like she'd smelled a decaying corpse. "What about Phoenix's ex? That formaldehyde sniffer asked for a divorce on Christmas day." She pointed at me with a bejeweled nail.

"Girl, I'm still amazed that after twenty years of marriage, the Casket King didn't give you corpse cooties." A shudder emphasized her point.

Gina picked up her glass and held it aloft. "I said, *decent person*."

"Speaking of Todd, I half-expected Joyce to be here tonight," Kat said. "She's almost an honorary Diva."

My stomach tumbled like an Olympic gymnast. "I didn't invite her."

"Why not?" Kat asked, her brow furrowed.

"I phoned Joyce to make arrangements to meet for dinner and to give her a Christmas present. For the past several months, Todd has whined to her about how I neglected him. I think she's also figured out that Todd and I will never reunite."

"So, what happened?" Kat asked.

"She blasted me for ruining her son's life."

Gina shot to her feet. "Didn't you tell her about his affairs?"

"It's not my place to tell her. She'll find out eventually," I said, rubbing my stomach.

Gina paced the room. "I can't believe this."

I signaled T for time out. "Enough about Todd and Joyce. It's complicated. Don't ruin my Christmas spirit."

Gina threw her hands in the air. She plopped back in her seat, mumbling under her breath.

Kat looked at me over the rim of her glass. "I wonder if we can find three ghosts to haunt Todd on Christmas Eve night like they did Scrooge?"

Gina chuckled. "I vote for those three angry women that he was having affairs with while he was married to Phoenix."

I groaned, covering my forehead with a hand. "Enough!"

Buffy raised her head and looked at me. It was the tone I used when she did something wrong.

"It's okay, Buffy. You're not in trouble," I said with a sing-song lilt.

Latishia scratched behind Buffy's long curly ears and crooned. "You're a good girl, aren't you?" She glanced up at me. "If you're so frazzled because you're dating two men, it's your own fault."

Kat put down her glass and leaned forward. "I don't understand. This seemed to be working out fine. What happened?"

I gripped the arms of my chair. "The schedule went haywire."

Gina laughed. "The what?"

"To be fair," I said, "Brent and Mike alternate Fridays and Saturdays for dates."

"What about Sunday?" Latishia asked as she stood to refill her wine glass with the last of the Jingle.

"They each get one Sunday a month."

Latishia returned to her seat and curled up. "Why?"

"One for each of them and two for me." I lowered the footrest of my recliner and stood. "Does anyone else want more Jingle?"

Kat and Gina raised their glasses. I walked to the kitchen to retrieve the backup pitcher from the fridge and returned to serve. None was left after I filled everyone's glasses.

Latishia scrutinized the empty vessel. "Good thing it's empty. I could drink my way to oblivion with that tasty concoction. The dry wine kept it from being too sweet."

I sat, popped the footrest back up, and sighed. "The problem is the holidays. Mike, Brent, and I are all having extra holiday events. It's messing with the schedule. I'm booked solid every evening through Christmas Eve!"

Gina's mouth dropped open. "Poor baby. Wish I had that problem."

"You think you do," I said. "I'm having problems finding time to think, let alone take care of my household obligations."

Gina drained her glass and plopped it down on the end table. "I think what we all need is another Diva getaway to escape our work and the men in our lives."

"I thought things were going well with Chris. Is he still planning to transfer to the Huntsville area?" I asked.

"It's taking *forever*. It's the pits when your guy lives out of town. Long-distance relationships lack certain physical aspects that I need. Chris and I discussed it. We decided not to be exclusive until he lives in this area."

I leaned forward. "I could use a vacation and time away from Mike and Brent. Mike is still pushing the idea of marriage, and I'm not there yet. I have a terrible feeling this whole situation is leading to some kind of huge decision on my part. When do y'all want to go?"

"Spring break!" Latishia said. "My cousin wants Dante to go to Gulf Shores with her family. She has two boys around his age."

Kat took a sip of her drink and sat it on the table. "That works for me. Jack is signed up for Space Camp. Since we live in Huntsville, he can do the day-camp version. My parents can drive him there and pick him up."

Gina nodded. "My caseload should slow up a bit by then. I'll be ready for a break. Where should we go?"

"Peru," I said with a huge grin.

"Peru!" the others chimed, slack-jawed.

"I watched a documentary about Peru yesterday. I was so intrigued that I did a little research. The exchange rate is three soles for every dollar. That makes for an inexpensive vacation. Besides, I want to see Machu Picchu while I'm still young enough to hike it."

Gina raised her glass. "Sounds adventurous. I'm in. To the land of the Incas!"

"The Incas," we toasted.

That is how our Diva adventure began.

CHAPTER 2: Brent

I ran down the to-do list and added a check mark beside stop the mail. *Why does preparing for a trip abroad always seem so hectic?*

I looked down at Buffy. "In two days, I'll arrive in Peru with your doggie aunts. You'll be vacationing with your doggie buddy next door." I pointed a finger at her. "Be a good girl, and remember, no accidents in the house."

The doorbell triggered Buffy into watchdog mode.

By the time I made it to the door, Brent was crooning sweet words to Buffy through the door, causing her stub of a tail to wiggle.

I opened the door, and Brent swept me into his arms and twirled. After a passionate kiss, he bent to pet Buffy. "How are my two beautiful ladies tonight?"

Buffy plopped on her back with a doggy grin, so he could rub her tummy.

After a brief rub, he straightened and smiled. "She'll let me do that all night. Are you ready for dinner?"

"Yep, let me grab my purse."

Brent opened the door to his new white Tesla Model Y, and I slid inside.

"How do you like the Y so far?" I asked, sniffing the new car smell.

"Love it. Maybe after you get back in the country, we can take a road trip and check out all the super chargers along the way." He fastened his seatbelt and put the car in reverse. My driveway appeared on the large monitor centered on the dash.

"Sounds fun, but I'll need to catch up at work first. Maybe June or September?"

"Great! Think about where you want to go and we can talk about it when you get back."

"This electric car is so quiet," I said.

He nodded. "One of the things I love about it."

We decided to eat at China Cook, a small Asian restaurant in Winchester Plaza. The parking lot was almost full, but we found a space further back.

After Brent helped me out of the car, he took my hand. It was warm. I always felt comfortable and safe with him.

The mingled scents of Chinese and Mexican food reached us in the parking lot. The Mexican restaurant next door looked busy.

China Cook was small and tastefully decorated. The far wall held cubbyholes filled with beautiful Asian objects. We strolled past a real-looking artificial tree that appeared to grow into the ceiling, while the hostess led us to our booth. Brent settled into the seat next to me.

The waitress appeared, took our drink orders, and left.

"Know what you want to order?" Brent asked, bumping my shoulder with his.

"Mongolian beef. It's one of my favorites." I bumped him back and smiled.

"I'm ordering happy family."

I perused the menu and found the dish. "Sounds good."

His knee moved against mine.

Sexy thoughts sped through my mind.

We ordered and settled back with our water. Soft music played in the background.

"I'm worried about you taking off to Peru." He ran his hand through his hair. "It's a Third World country."

I sighed and took his hand. "It's not like I'm traveling alone. I'll be with the Divas. Peru Tourism will have English speaking guides with us, and they're providing all the transportation."

His shoulders lowered a bit. "That's good, but what about the hotels?"

"We're booked into four-star hotels, which are on the good side of town," I said.

Brent nodded. "That makes me feel better." He unwrapped his flatware. "Will the tour guide meet you at the airport in Peru?"

"That's what they told us." I squeezed his hand. "Don't worry so much."

He put his arm around me and squeezed. "Can't help it."

Hoping to guide the conversation away from the trip, I asked, "How's your dad doing?"

"He's recovering. Lucky for him the heart attack was mild. His doc referred him to a clinic that treats COPD. He can already tell the difference in how he feels."

"Wonderful." I braced myself to ask a more sensitive question. "How's your mom?"

He rolled his eyes. "Mom is extra clingy right now. Dad's heart attack rocked her already unsteady world. She's driving the family batshit crazy. My sister's avoiding her calls." He leaned toward me and lowered his voice. "It's awful to say, but I pray when the time comes, they go together, or that Dad outlives her."

Our meals arrived, giving us a good excuse not to continue the conversation about his parents. We shared each other's dinner and discussed his work and all the sights the Divas would see in Peru.

Rubbing our distended stomachs, we asked our waitress for take-out containers before we opened the fortune cookies she'd placed on the table.

The crinkling plastic wrapper finally gave way, releasing the almond and butter scent of the cookie. I cracked the crisp morsel open and pulled out the small rectangular paper nestled inside. "Mine says, *Great adventures await you.* What does your fortune predict?"

"*Something unexpected is in your future.*" He tilted his head. "I wonder if it will be good or bad?"

"Or both. I'm hoping it's good." I said, winking.

Brent paid the bill while I placed the leftovers in containers to carry home.

When we stepped into the parking lot, I shivered and pulled my coat collar closer around my throat.

Brent opened the frunk, the small trunk where the engine would reside in an internal combustion vehicle, and nested the leftovers among the charging cables.

He opened my door, and I was greeted by a blast of warm air.

"How is the car already warm inside?" I asked, snuggling into the warm seat.

Brent bent and kissed me. "I turned on the seat warmers and climate control while I was paying. I couldn't let you sit in a chilly car."

We held hands while driving to my home. He started kissing me the moment we closed the front door. Within minutes, he'd picked me up and carried me to the bedroom.

I lost myself in the passion of his lingering kisses and skillful hands. Our sensual lovemaking grew more intense with our need. My desire to connect to this man was strong, because I wouldn't see him for many days. I'd miss him.

Our muscles tensed with pleasure before we collapsed. Sated, we fell asleep in each other's arms.

Early the next morning, we had a quick, playful romp, and cuddled for a while. He lay on his back, my head on his shoulder.

"I'm gonna miss you a lot this time," Brent said, his brow furrowed.

We'd only just begun dating when I traveled to the beach with the Divas. I propped myself on one elbow and asked, "Why?"

"You're an important part of my life."

I snuggled back onto his shoulder and smiled. I traced patterns in his chest hair. "Glad to hear it. I'll miss you, too."

He gazed into my eyes. "Seriously, text me once a day so I'll know you're okay."

"Only if you'll text me with any important news," I said, snuggling closer. The man was like a furnace. My personal body warmer.

Brent chuckled. "Don't bring a tornado back from vacation, like the Divas did last time."

"That wasn't us." I gave him a little shove. "The Divas are a force, but not a force of nature."

He laughed with a twinkle in his eyes. "I'm not so sure about that."

I lay tight against him, my eyes closed. *Do I love Brent? I know he cares about me, but does he love me? Maybe this trip and time away from him will give me some answers.*

CHAPTER 3: Mike

Mike picked me up for our dinner date the day before the trip. I closed my office door and moved into his arms.

"My Darling Fish Lips, you look lovely tonight." He leaned over and kissed me.

"Thanks." I reached up and wiped my favorite lip color off his mouth.

He took my hand and led me to his Jeep. "I'll drive. No use taking two cars." He opened the door for me. "Let's go to Jim and Nick's. I'm in the mood for barbecue."

I climbed up to the seat and buckled my seatbelt. "Sounds tasty."

The heavy traffic on University Drive was stop and go. When we drove past the Olive Garden, I noticed the parking lot was packed.

"I hope Jim and Nick's isn't too busy. I'm hungry." My growling stomach confirmed my declaration.

"Me, too. I've been thinking about those giant barbecue baked potatoes all day."

"There's no way I can tackle one of those," I said, laughing. "I ordered one several months back. It provided three meals for me."

The parking lot looked full, but we found a space behind the building. Mike helped me down from the vehicle, took my hand, and led me at a brisk pace toward the entrance.

"Let's get in line."

I huffed puffs of steam while almost running. *Good grief, this is March, not February. Where's spring?*

We were soon seated in a wooden booth along the back wall. Mike slid in opposite me. The smell of smoked meat, tangy sauce, and onion rings permeated the establishment, triggering my stomach to rumble again.

I looked over the menu. Everything looked delicious. "I'm having a pork sandwich with fries."

"Sounds good," he said.

The waitress took our drink orders. Ten minutes later, she set a Corona in front of Mike, gave me a sweating glass of sweet iced tea, and plopped a basket of their tiny cheese muffins in the center of the wooden table.

"Ooh, I love these." I reached for one of the tasty treats.

Mike scrunched his face. "Too sweet for me."

"Good, that leaves more for me." I flashed a playful grin before popping one in my mouth and chewed. "Yum."

Mike's brow furrowed. From out of nowhere, he asked, "Do you still insist on going on this blasted trip with *those Divas* to Peru?"

The emphasis on *those Divas* didn't escape my attention. "Yep." I picked up another cheese muffin. "I can't wait to see Machu Picchu." I ate the treat and smiled. "The whole trip is planned, and the flights, hotels, tours, and guides were prepaid."

"I was hoping you'd forget all this nonsense." He grimaced before trying for a more pleasant tone. "Wouldn't you rather go to a civilized place, like Paris?"

I sat back and wiped my hands with the thick paper napkin. "I'd love to go to Paris someday. Maybe we can arrange a trip later this year, or maybe next year."

He harrumphed, crossing his arms. "You're so stubborn."

"I'm stubborn!" I sat back and copied his posture. "You're the most stubborn man I've ever met."

A young woman clutching menus glanced our way before leading a family of four past us to a nearby table. The parents chattered to the hostess. The two teens followed, never lifting their gazes from their phones.

When I turned my attention back to Mike, he scowled at me before taking a swill from his beer.

What's wrong with him? The closer this trip gets, the grumpier he becomes. I reached across and squeezed his hand. "What happened to the sweet guy I met in Florida?"

He shifted in his seat and looked down.

Insight flashed on. "Wait a minute, do you think I'm going to Peru to hook up with a guy?"

He glared at me. "That's what you did on your Florida vacation with *those Divas*."

I realized my mouth was hanging open and closed it. Taking a deep breath to clear my mind, I exhaled and said, "I went to Florida with my *friends* to recover from my Dad's death and a divorce. I wasn't looking for a guy."

"From what I heard, you had a date with some colonel and then found me. How do I know you don't plan to add a new guy to your harem?"

Harem! Heat bloomed in my gut and spread across my body, sending a plume of internal fire toward my head in the form of a blistering hot flash. I dabbed moisture from my face with the napkin.

"For your information, I had nothing to do with that situation. Aaron set up Gina and me with blind dates. We were opposed to the idea, but Latishia and Kat wanted us to have dinner as a group."

Mike sat back and crossed his arms again. The muscle at his jaw spasmed.

Feeling falsely accused, I said, "I didn't pick you up. I was reading in the hotel lobby, when *you* barged in on me."

A tall guy with red hair placed a humongous potato that filled a platter in front of Mike, and a plate with a sandwich and golden fries in front of me.

"Does everything look good?" he asked, grinning.

"Fine." Mike said, his narrow-eyed glare focused on me.

My stomach tumbled. I picked up a fry and crammed it into my mouth. It was crunchy, salty, and delicious. *I refuse to let him ruin my meal.*

Mike focused on the potato, piled high with butter, cheese, sour cream, and shredded pork, and ignored me.

We ate in silence, avoiding all eye contact. I fumed over his accusation.

Our waitress returned after we'd finished. "Do y'all want dessert?" She reached to remove Mike's empty platter and then piled my plate on top.

Before I could answer, Mike said, "No. Give me the bill."

We stared at each other across the table, the air thick with tension. I wasn't sure what I could say that wouldn't worsen the situation.

The waitress returned five minutes later with the check.

Mike threw some bills on top of the check, stood, and pushed his wallet into his back pocket. "Let's go."

He didn't take my hand, but instead stomped like a petulant teen toward his car. He opened my door and almost slammed it shut on my coat.

I'd barely fastened my seatbelt when he screeched out of the parking lot and zoomed onto University Drive. Stiff with fear, I jammed my foot on the nonexistent brake pedal and clutched whatever was available while he sped back to my office.

He slammed to a stop in my office parking lot, throwing me against the unforgiving seat restraint.

I turned to confront his driving, but clamped my mouth shut. His face was red and contorted with anger.

Good grief, if he doesn't calm down, he'll stroke out. I unbuckled my seatbelt, ready to escape the situation.

In a gruff tone, Mike said, "Do you insist on going on this trip with *those women*?"

I gripped the door handle. "Yes. *Those women* are my best friends. Thanks for dinner." I opened the door, slid out, and strode toward my Prius with clenched fists.

A roaring engine and squealing tires alerted me to jump to the side, before Mike barreled past and out the parking lot.

I hurried to my car, jumped inside, and locked the doors. While resting my forehead on the steering wheel, I tried to deep-breathe my pounding heart to a slower rate.

I sat up and swiped a tear from my cheek. "I can't believe any of that happened." Trembling from the adrenaline aftermath, I drove home to complete my last-minute pre-trip preparations.

At nine o'clock, Mike's ring tone blared from my phone. I stood glaring at it, remembering the dinner fiasco. Anger bloomed in my gut, spreading like acid through my veins. I turned and walked back to the suitcase I was packing.

A few minutes later he phoned again.

Closing my eyes, I heaved a frustrated sigh. "Give me a break." After running my hands through my hair, I told myself, "Be an adult, Phoenix. Don't leave town with this conflict unresolved. What if he died or something?" I reached for the phone.

"I'm sorry," Mike blurted. "I behaved badly. Can you forgive me?"

My gut cramped. *I need to think about this incident some more.* Several red flags were waving in my mind.

"I'll try. I need some time and space to settle down. Let's talk about it when I get back."

"Can't we talk now?" he asked.

"It's late, I'm tired, and my flight leaves early in the morning."

"Please forgive me. I want us to marry." He pleaded.

"This isn't a good time. I appreciate the apology, but I'm still upset. Your driving scared the crap out of me. It wasn't safe."

"I'm so sorry. Can I please come over so we can talk?" he asked with a desperate tone.

On a hunch, I walked to my home office on the other side of the house, and peeked out the window. Mike's Jeep sat in the driveway.

My jaw tightened. "I know you're parked in my drive. Nothing productive will come out of a discussion tonight. Go home. I'll see you when I get back."

CHAPTER 4: The Journey Begins

My first inkling that my travel plans were going haywire hit when I rolled my luggage to the airline check-in desk at the Huntsville International Airport. I was the first of the Hot Flash Divas to arrive. This surprised me, since Kat's the early-bird in our foursome.

No one staffed the airline counter. I glanced down the way. All the other airline desks were manned and had people in a queue. I turned when I heard someone coming up behind me.

It was Kat, wearing a backpack and pulling a large suitcase. "Phoenix, are you ready for our big South American adventure?" She pushed her glasses back in place with her index finger before doing a salsa step in place. "Peru, here we come."

"Not if someone from this airline doesn't check us in," I said, lifting my hair off my shoulders for ventilation. Heat rose up my core toward my neck and face. *Dang hot flash.*

"I can't believe no one's working this desk." Kat tucked one side of her hair behind an ear while looking for our missing clerk.

Gina rolled her London Fog bag behind Kat and cocked a hip. "I see Latishia's late again." Her gaze tracked a tall blond man who approached the Delta counter.

"She's probably having trouble getting her bag to close." Kat chuckled. "You know how she loves to overpack."

Gina fluffed her curls while watching the object of her interest. "I wonder if she'll be able to stick to a fifty-five pound bag, or if she'll pay big-time to bring a second one?"

Kat rolled her eyes. "All we need is another situation like Florida." She shifted her weight and crossed her arms. "If she brings a separate case for her clothes and shoes, I won't be helping her haul them through these airports."

"Me, either," I said. "This isn't a fashion event. I only brought four pairs of shoes." I ticked them off on my fingers. "Hiking boots, walking shoes, dress pumps, and a pair of sandals to wear in the room or at the pool."

Kat pointed. "We'll soon find out. I think that's her coming in the door."

Latishia pulled one of her signature hot-pink suitcases behind her and had donned a matching backpack.

"Phew!" She fanned herself. "The only thing I hate more than hot flashes are airports. I despise flying. The seats are too small. The last time I flew was in 1985." She glanced around. "Why are we standing here?"

I stepped to the side and swept my hand toward the empty counter.

"Huh." Latishia whipped around, sending her long braids flying. "Every other airline has a ticket agent."

"We noticed," Gina said.

Ten minutes later, a petite woman with dark hair rushed past me. She slid behind the counter and struggled out of her coat. I scrunched my nose at the stink of cigarette smoke that drifted in her wake. Behind us, eight more people now stood in line.

"Give me a minute to get the computers up," the agent said. "I have to use both of them to check you in."

Latishia harrumphed and crossed her arms. She gave the woman her famous stink-eye.

The ticket agent hustled back and forth between the two computers for ten more minutes before asking for my name, and later for my ID.

She typed away and frowned. After shuffling over to the other computer, she typed some more. The frown deepened to a scowl.

"Uh, oh," Latishia mumbled.

The agent printed out the boarding passes for the three flights: Silver Airways to Orlando, Florida, American Airlines to Miami, and Latam Airlines to Lima, Peru.

"Did you know your luggage won't be transferred onto the last flight?" the agent asked.

"It should be," I said, feeling a trickle of dread.

She shook her head. "You'll have to pick it up at the baggage claim area in Miami, and then recheck it."

My shoulders stiffened. "I only have a fifty-minute layover at the Miami airport."

"I'm sorry. There's nothing I can do about it."

Since we'd all booked our flights with the same online travel site, we had the same luggage transfer problem. My mind buzzed trying to find a possible solution, but none surfaced. The agent repeated the back and forth routine between the two computers until all four of us were checked in. We shouldered our backpacks and made our way to the escalators that led to security.

Gina said, "I need coffee. I'd normally have two cups by now."

"Hot tea would be nice," Kat said.

Latishia wiped her brow with her forearm. "I don't know about y'all, but I could drink a gallon of water."

Security in Huntsville was a breeze for Kat and me because we had star IDs. I travel a good bit and know the drill.

Not so for Gina and Latishia. The very sight of the security area triggered a hot flash for Latishia. "None of this was here the last time I flew." She broke into a sweat, attracting a beady-eyed glare from one of the TSA agents.

"Thank the terrorists," I said.

It took Gina two tries to make it through the scanner because she forgot to remove her new Apple watch.

Latishia, fists planted on her hips, complained about removing her shoes to a TSA agent. "Mind you, my feet don't stink, but one of these days, you'll have someone knock you flat on your butt from their vile foot odor."

The agent smirked.

The first time Latishia set off the alarm on the scanner, she stopped and looked around wild-eyed. "Why is this thing buzzing at me?"

A security person pointed at her Apple watch.

Mumbling under her breath, she went back and took off her watch. Latishia walked back through again.

Buzz!

She flapped her arms in frustration. "It's doing it again!" She glared at the machine.

A different security person said, "Please make sure you remove *all* your jewelry."

Latishia rolled her eyes. She walked back through and took off her earrings, three rings, three bangle bracelets, and a necklace. Her lower lip protruded into one of her famous pouts. "This better work."

The scanner alarmed again.

Latishia's shoulders slumped.

An official-looking female officer approached her with a wand.

Latishia took a step back, eyeing the device. She shot a look at me. "Why is she coming at me with that thing?"

"It's a body scanner." I felt her angst. I'd been scanned several times with a wand during my travels. It was embarrassing. Everyone stopped and looked at me like I was wearing explosives.

The closer the officer came, the rounder Latishia's eyes became. She looked ready to run.

Kat stood beside me, biting her lip to keep from laughing. I knew her past travels had also included some humorous wand issues.

The female officer waved the wand around Latishia. It went crazy every time it came near her impressive bosom.

"Ma'am, do you have anything stuffed in your bra?" the security agent asked.

Latishia threw her shoulders back. "Just the girls."

"Are you wearing an underwire bra?"

"Of course. Don't you wear one for support?"

The female guard, whose bosom was equivalent to two mosquito bites, shook her head and waved her through. It took a while for Latishia to put herself back together. I already felt exhausted, and we hadn't left Huntsville. Sighing, I sank into a seat at the assigned gate to await our flight. I gave serious thought to coffee, but a long line snaked around the snack shop. Due to the delayed check-in and the fiasco in the security line, we no longer had time to purchase drinks.

Gina dropped her backpack onto the seat next to me. "Kat, what does Dr. Howard think about this new coronavirus in China?"

"Doc told me if China is any indication, this could be a big problem world-wide. He's old friends with Dr. Anthony Fauci, the Director of NIAID. They've been communicating about this for weeks. Based on everything he's learned, Dr. Howard believes this could be our next pandemic, and he doesn't think our country is ready."

Latishia leaned forward, "What's NIAID?"

Kat smiled. "Sorry, it's the acronym for the National Institute of Allergy and Infectious Diseases."

"Good grief. I'd like a vacation where I don't have to worry about bad news." I rubbed the back of my neck. "I've enough problems trying to decide between Mike and Brent. I was hoping time away from them would clear my mind."

Kat zipped her fanny pack closed. "You've been dating them for what, six months? Why do you feel you have to decide between them now?"

"For one thing, Mike is pushing harder to get married."

"Nothing new there," Gina said. "The man was ready to put a ring on your finger a month after you met him."

"Maybe it's me. I'm changing. After Todd asked for a divorce, I was in a complete emotional shutdown. Lately, my feelings have started peeking out like crocus in the spring. A relationship with two willing men was great for a while. Now I'm confused. I'm not sure where this is going." I rolled my eyes. "Then there was last night."

"What happened last night?" Kat asked, shifting her backpack to a nearby seat.

I described my date with Mike.

Kat's brows shot up. "Mike? I thought he was a good guy." She shook her head. "A man with a temper that hot is dangerous."

Gina leaned closer. "I agree with Kat. He could've killed you both by driving like a maniac."

"I bet he showed up at your house hoping for some makeup sex before you left town," Latishia said, adjusting her earring.

"Well, he didn't get any," I said.

"Sounds like this vacation is just what we both need," said Latishia. "I need some time away from Aaron. He acts like engagement means we have to bolt down to the courthouse and tie the knot tomorrow. He and Dante are doing better, but I think they need more time to adjust to each other."

"I agree. Don't let him rush you," I said. "I'd like to issue a challenge. Let's take a break from the news on our phones. Only text messages from our family and loved ones. We can't change what happens in the world while we're in Peru."

Kat sucked her bottom lip. "It might be good to take a break from the world and its problems. I'm in, as long as I can check on Jack and my parents with texts."

"Me, too." Gina yawned so wide that her jaw popped. "The influx of post-holiday divorce cases seemed worse than usual this year. I need a break from bad news."

"Just texts are fine with me. I don't want to look at any business emails either," said Latishia. "Life in Decatur won't fall apart if one of my building loans gets delayed."

We high-fived each other and settled back into our seats.

The agent announced we were ready to board.

Once we were on the small plane, I saw a side of Kat I'd never witnessed before. She pulled a small packet of disinfectant wipes from her backpack and wiped down the armrests, tray tables, and any other surface that she and Latishia would touch.

"Wow," Gina said, grinning. "I didn't know you were such a germophobe. You didn't behave this way when we drove to Florida last year."

Kat looked up and frowned. "I read a study which found that airplane tray tables had more bacteria per square inch than toilet flush handles."

Gina cocked her head. "Yeah, what kind?"

"Cold viruses, flu viruses, norovirus, and MRSA."

I exchanged a glance with Gina. "Can we borrow one of those wipes?"

When she finished sanitizing, Kat took the window seat across the aisle from us.

Latishia squashed her roundness into the undersized seat next to her. "Dang seats are smaller than I remembered."

The flight from Huntsville to Orlando on the small plane was noisy, so I plugged in my noise-canceling earphones and closed my eyes. I tried to ignore the impending luggage disaster that loomed over us like a thunderhead, threatening doom.

My argument with Mike had kept me awake a good part of the night before. I drifted toward sleep.

Gina jabbed me with a pointy elbow.

I rubbed my side and pulled off my earphones. "Do you sharpen those bony elbows every night?"

Her eyes narrowed. "Have you ever been to Miami's airport? It's huge! There's no way we're going to make it out of the plane in time to claim our luggage, recheck it, and make it back through security."

Kat leaned across Latishia. "We could try to get it fixed in Orlando, but the layover is so short."

Latishia said, "I don't want to go through a long security line again at the Orlando airport. I'm still traumatized from the last one. I swear, I thought that woman was going to strip search me."

Thirty minutes later, we deplaned in Orlando. I was happy to leave the crowded aircraft. After a quick pit stop, Gina and I purchased several packs of disinfectant wipes at a kiosk. We had to hightail it across the airport to reach the correct gate for our next flight. There was no time to talk to a ticket agent, let alone go back through security.

So far, so good. We made it to our next flight.

The large, sleek American Airlines jet going to Miami made the previous plane look like an awkward adolescent. We passed through four sections on the way back to the fifth row from the rear of the plane. After stowing our gear, we manically cleaned our seats and tray tables.

A tall Jamaican flight attendant assigned to our area winked at me and said, "Girl, I love your hair. What do you call that color?"

"Ginger," I said.

He lowered his voice. "Is it natural?"

Latishia looked up from her cleaning. "She's a true natural redhead."

He grinned at Latishia. "Lucky her."

I wiggled my finger for him to come closer. I indicated the four of us with a sweep of my hand. "We have a luggage issue. We need your help."

"I'll try." He winked again.

I explained our problem. "As you can see, we're seated at the back of this plane. If we have to wait our turn to get off, we won't have a chance to claim our baggage and recheck it."

"Let me discuss it with my colleagues." He grinned, showing bright white teeth. "We'll see what we can do?"

Twenty minutes later, he returned. "I'm allowed to tell you the baggage turnstile number before you leave the plane. According to the rules, I can't give you special treatment on exiting the plane." He leaned closer and whispered, "When we land, get your carry-ons down and be ready to move. I'll make a poof sound on the microphone. When I do, hightail it down to the front so you can deplane first."

My shoulder muscles loosened with relief. *How difficult can it be to grab a bag and recheck it?* I listened to an audiobook and enjoyed the rest of the flight.

CHAPTER 5: The Race

The jet bounced to a landing. We wrestled our backpacks and purses from under our seats and secured them in our laps, ready to leap into action. I could feel the minutes ticking past, as the pilot taxied for what seemed like an hour. After an eon, the plane eased close to the gate and stopped.

"Poof."

Gina stood, moved into the aisle, and whispered, "You go first."

I rose and started down the aisle with Gina behind me. Kat and Latishia brought up the rear. Latishia, lush with padding, kept saying, "Sorry. Excuse me."

When I arrived at the front, the steward shooed me into the first-class kitchen area. I backed in as far as possible. The rest piled in front of me. Latishia, who was last, did her best to scoot out of sight, but her giant boobs still poked past the doorway. The airline employee trying to line up the mobile passage to the door was on his third try. His panicked expression said it all.

"Come on!" I mumbled.

Tick tock.

The Jamaican steward opened the plane's door and waved us out. We shot like a cork from a pop gun and ran down the chute.

Once in the Miami airport, we craned our necks, trying to find the baggage claim sign.

Kat pointed to her right. "There it is." She took off with surprising speed for such a tiny person.

While speed walking behind her, I noticed her backpack was black with white polka dots. The zipper pocket was a smiling cat face with silver glitter ears. I grinned. *Interesting backpack.*

I ran to catch up. "Where did you find your backpack?"

Kat glanced over. "Christmas present from Jack."

"Your kid has a sense of humor." I looked back. Gina wasn't far behind us, but Latishia was losing ground.

None of the people movers were working. Following Kat, I swerved to pass anyone walking slower than me. Every time I thought we were close, there would be another sign pointing for us to continue.

I slowed to struggle out of my backpack's straps so I could pull off my jacket. A hot flash bubbled inside me like lava in an angry volcano. I dabbed at sweat forming on my brow.

Kat pulled ahead.

Looking back, I noticed that Gina lagged, her face florid and covered with sweat. Latisha trudged along in the distance. Bless her heart, she seemed ready to drop.

I yelled back to Gina. "You've been here before. How far is this baggage claim area? Two miles?"

Gina shrugged. "I don't remember."

I forged on. I'd lost sight of Kat, but saw a baggage sign pointing down some stairs. After hurrying down, I saw the baggage claim area. *At last!*

Kat stood examining the monitor, her chest heaving. She looked in my direction and waved me over. She pointed at the closest revolving rack. "It's this one."

I braced my hands on my knees, hung my head, and gulped air until I was no longer light-headed. Then I straightened and stretched to pop my back. "Jeez, I need to work out more. I wonder how many folks die from a heart attack while trying to claim their luggage."

Kat wiped her damp forehead. "I go to the gym three times a week and I'm struggling."

The luggage carousel groaned as it began to rotate.

Gina trudged in our direction and stopped beside me. The fluorescent lights highlighted the sheen of perspiration on her face.

"Are you okay?" I asked.

Through gritted teeth, she said, "I feel the need to sue somebody."

"Calm down," I said. "You look ready to stroke out. Can't sue anyone from the grave."

Kat and I had wrestled our suitcases from the moving belt by the time Latishia huffed her way to join us. When her hot pink bag came within reach, she gave a mighty heave, nearly falling over. Her glistening face looked purple, and her bosom rose and fell with the effort of breathing.

We all were sweating and worse for wear. Latishia looked near collapse. Gina's red face looked ready to explode. Even Kat was still breathing hard.

I covered my still-racing heart with a hand and took deep breaths to slow my heart rate. When I felt better, I said, "Who would guess we needed to be marathon runners to get to the baggage claim area? Let's go."

We found the correct stairs to take us to the airline check-in area. My calves burned by the time I reached the top. We rushed past a large American Airlines section and sped past airline after airline, many of which I'd never heard of before. Latam was still nowhere in sight. It was a reverse journey of what seemed like a mile.

Ten minutes later, Kat spotted a woman in a Latam uniform and waved us in that direction. We rolled our cases over to her. Between gasps, Kat handed the woman her boarding pass and asked, "Are we... in the right place?"

With a Hispanic accent, the agent said, "You need to check-in at American."

In a strident tone, I said, "What do you mean? The ticket says, Latam!"

Gina muttered, "Merda," and sank to sit on her luggage.

Soaked with sweat, I glanced over at Gina, who'd been my friend since Parochial school. When she starts cursing in Italian, her fiery temper is close to rupturing. I couldn't speak for the other Divas, but I felt like crying.

The agent tried to explain the situation, but it made no sense, and we didn't have time to debate the airline's policy. We turned, rushed back toward American Airlines, and sped past Latishia.

Kat waved for her to follow. "Wrong way. Follow us."

Latishia reversed directions.

It was a long way. When we arrived, Kat rushed forward to an open clerk who had Lucy printed on her name tag. She handed Lucy her boarding pass and heaved her suitcase onto the device to have it weighed. Then she collapsed against the counter.

Lucy typed and pursed her lips. Her eyes flicked from one side of the screen to another as a line formed between her brows.

I glanced back, trying to spot my friends. Sweat trickled down my sides.

Gina stumbled to a stop next to me, her unruly curls sticking out from her head like springs.

"Where's Latishia?" I asked.

She turned to look behind her. Multitudes of people passed back and forth. "She was behind me a moment ago. Geez, I feel like my heart is using my ribs for drums."

A motorized cart eased to a stop near us, and Latishia climbed out. The man handed her the pink suitcase.

I was about to congratulate her for finding a ride, when Kat said, "What do you mean we can't make this flight?"

Lucy looked up. "There's more traveling in your party?"

The rest of us raised our hands and rushed the counter. I'm sure we all had desperate expressions.

Using her attorney tone, Gina asked, "Why can't we make this flight? It hasn't left yet."

Lucy said, "You might make it through security in time to board. That's not the problem. You needed to be here twenty minutes ago to get your luggage on the flight. You and your luggage are required to fly on the same plane."

I grumbled, "One more thing we can thank the terrorists for messing up."

Lucy typed away on the keyboard. Her frown deepened. "The next flight I can get you using Latam will be in two days."

"Two days! But we have tours starting at two o'clock tomorrow afternoon," I whined. An adolescent couldn't have done better.

"How did this happen?" Lucy asked with a sympathetic tone. Her gaze took in our disheveled clothing and sweat-streaked faces.

I stepped forward and explained the whole debacle.

Lucy nodded her understanding as her fingers flew across the keyboard. Ten minutes later, she said, "I can fly you to Dallas-Fort Worth on American, and from there, you can catch an American flight to Peru." She cocked a brow. "There is one problem."

My gut somersaulted.

"Instead of arriving in Peru at eleven tonight, you'll land at six tomorrow morning. Will that work?"

I looked at the Divas, who all nodded. "Yes," I said. "Please book it, and thank you."

We sagged against the counter. I'm not sure if it was relief or exhaustion or maybe both.

Lucy handed us boarding passes and pointed to her right. "You need to head straight to security because your flight leaves in thirty minutes."

We grabbed our luggage claim receipts and raced toward security.

I adjusted the slipping strap on my backpack without slowing down and thought, *What else could go wrong?*

This time, it appeared that Latishia was determined to do anything to avoid being wanded by a TSA agent. The Miami airport, unlike Huntsville, had x-ray machines. I made it through with no problems and turned to watch Latishia enter the device. She raised her arms and closed her eyes.

"You're clear to go through, Ma'am," the security agent said.

I sighed with relief. *Thank you, God.* I leaned a forearm on Kat's shoulder. "I won't feel at ease until we board the plane."

"Me, either," Kat said, pushing up her glasses. "This luggage fiasco has about done me in."

By the time we reached the gate, my legs felt like rope, and I was a sticky mess. My Apple Watch buzzed on my wrist. Thinking it was a text message, I looked down. I'd closed my exercise ring.

The announcement blasting over the intercom didn't ease my anxiety.

"Ladies and gentlemen, we are overbooked on this flight. We are asking for volunteers to take a flight leaving tomorrow. You will receive a hundred-dollar credit and a complimentary hotel stay."

The four of us looked at each other.

I leaned close and whispered, "I think we're the reason they're overbooked." I felt a twinge of guilt.

Gina jutted her chin forward. "Hell and high water aren't keeping me from boarding that plane. I'll sue them for millions if they try to stop me."

From the expression in her dark eyes, I knew Gina meant it.

We found seats in the boarding area and sank into them. I texted Peru Tourism about our luggage problem and flight changes. The confirmation text felt reassuring. "Okay, Peru Tourism knows about the shift in our flights."

The agent continued to seek volunteers by upping the money rebate.

Kat rubbed her temples. "If we didn't have a tour scheduled, I'd take that last deal."

Once again, we were one of the last groups to board. We squeezed down the aisles of the giant plane carrying our backpacks and purses. We were seated in the same section, but not next to each other. We brandished our disinfectant wipes and began cleaning. I received a few incredulous looks, but I didn't care. I didn't want to be sick on our vacation. Thanks to Kat, I couldn't look at an unwiped tray table without feeling squirmy.

I settled into my seat, buckled up, and took a deep breath to release the last of my pent-up frustration. *We're on the plane. Everything will go smooth as glass from this point forward.* I put on my noise-canceling earphones and turned on my audiobook.

CHAPTER 6: Peru or Bust

I staggered off the plane in Dallas-Fort Worth and flexed my legs, trying to ease the tingling sensation. Once I felt more stable, I checked my ticket to search for the next flight number.

Most of the seats at the gate were full of passengers waiting to board the plane we'd left. The area buzzed with activity. I joined Kat, who peered at a row of monitors suspended from the ceiling. She walked over to an airline employee and showed her ticket. "Excuse me, but where is this gate?"

"It's in the international section." He pointed. "That way. Follow the signs."

"I don't believe it," I said. My shoulders sagged.

Gina stifled a yawn. "Believe what?"

"Another long walk," Kat said.

Latishia yawned, too. "Good Lord, I didn't know I needed to go into training to make my way through an airport." She glared at Gina. "Stop yawning. I'm doing it now."

Gina crossed her arms and glowered. "Well, excuse me."

I held up my hands. "Ladies, we're tired. Calm down and follow me. At least we don't need to run to the next gate."

It took a while, but we found the gate and settled into the nearest group of four seats.

The entire day had been exhausting. If I didn't do something to amuse myself, I feared I'd fall asleep. The psychologist in me divided the people occupying the area into categories. There were the slouchers, who seemed to melt into their seats. The techies sat around any available plug that would allow them to charge and work on their devices. The pacers were the antsiest. They wandered from shop to shop or circled the area like vultures. The mothers wore harried looks while negotiating, threatening, and herding their children back to their seats.

Gina's elbow poked me. "Categorizing people again?"

"Who, me?"

She smirked. "You've been doing it since the first grade."

Kat leaned closer. "What's Phoenix doing?"

Gina stretched and yawned again. "She categorizes people wherever she goes. Put her in a crowded room, and ten minutes later, she'll have everyone organized into her system."

"Tell us your categories for this international mass of humanity," Latishia said while dabbing her face with a tissue. "I need all the entertainment I can get."

I pointed out each group. My friends observed for several moments.

Latishia pointed toward a section of seats on the fringe of the area where several folks were eating. "You missed one. Those are the snackers."

"Good category. Every airport has them," I said.

Gina shoved her phone into her large purse. "Two years ago when my family traveled to Italy, you'd have thought they were afraid of starvation. My aunt Rosie packed a large antipasto tray. They passed it over the seats and down the aisle, making sure no one went hungry."

Latishia smacked her lips. "I want to travel with your family next time. Why didn't you bring one of those trays?"

Gina shrugged. "I'm not Aunt Rosie." She giggled. "Can you imagine me carrying a meat and cheese tray while I ran through Miami's airport?"

We chuckled.

I glanced at my watch. "If we'd made our flight, we would be landing in Lima in two hours."

Gina scrubbed her face with her hands and looked over at me with bleary eyes. "Don't remind me. I only hope I can sleep on the plane."

Kat stretched, causing her back to pop. "I'll feel better when we're seated on the plane, our luggage is onboard, and we're in the air."

Gina made the sign of the cross and pointed up. "From your lips to God's ears."

An announcement to board our flight blared over the intercom.

CHAPTER 7: Peru at Last

The flight attendants milling about woke me the next morning. I tried to open my eyes, but they felt like some prankster had super-glued them shut. I rubbed them and blinked. My tongue felt dry and swollen. *I feel like I'm in a desert, instead of on a large plane.* I pulled my contact wetting solution from the red backpack at my feet. Stumbling on tingling legs, I headed toward the restroom to rewet my lenses.

When I returned, I was pleased to see a beverage cart coming my way. The attendant handed out bottles of water and assured us breakfast would soon be served.

I settled into my seat and chugged down the water. By the time I felt somewhat hydrated, the breakfast cart had arrived.

After consuming a blueberry muffin and coffee, I felt fortified to venture into a foreign country where Spanish was spoken and where I'd read we couldn't drink the water.

The landing at Lima's Jorge Chávez International Airport was smooth. We gathered our belongings and waited.

Relieved to be on the runway, I flipped my hair over my shoulder and said, "We're in Lima. I can hardly believe we made it."

Gina yawned. "I can't wait to see the city."

Latishia stretched with her hands over her head before rolling her shoulders.

The guy across the aisle stared open-mouthed at her breasts. I expected him to say "mommy" and try to grab them. The small-breasted woman sitting next to him sent her elbow into his ribs. *That must be his wife*, I thought. *She's not putting up with his behavior.* I grinned. *Good for her.*

A voice over the intercom announced, "Would everyone please be seated. We have a medical emergency. If there is a doctor on this flight, would you please report to the first-class section?"

A groan of frustration moved through the cabin like the wave at a football game.

Kat stood and eased toward the aisle. "I may be able to help." She took off toward the front of the plane.

A nearby passenger gawked and asked, "Is she a doctor?"

"Nurse," Gina said.

The cabin filled with conversation that waxed and waned in volume. Thirty long minutes later, Kat came back into view.

"What's going on?" Latishia asked. "I'm hungry. Hobbits had a good idea when they invented the second breakfast."

"An older man had a heart attack. Fortunately for him, there was a doctor in the first-class section. The paramedics already have him on a gurney and are taking him off the plane."

Fifteen minutes later, we were allowed to deplane. It was a slow, frustrating shuffle down the narrow aisle while struggling to keep our backpacks and purses from snagging on the seats.

Craning my neck to see over the crowd, I said, "I hope our tour guide is here to meet us." The way things were going, it would be the final blow to my exhausted psyche if we were stuck at the airport with no guide.

Our first stop was the ladies' room. Gina pointed at a large roll of toilet paper hanging on a dispenser near the sinks. "Are we supposed to get our paper there?"

"I don't know, but I'm not taking any chances," I said as I rolled some off.

I entered the stall, wiped the seat, and pulled out one of my travel toilet-seat covers from my purse. A sign written in Spanish and English said, ¡DO NOT THROW PAPER INTO THE TOILET! THROW IN THE TRASH CAN. There next to the commode stood a plastic container with crumpled used paper inside. The smell of human waste gagged me.

I shuddered. *Yuck!* "Did y'all read the sign on the door?" I asked.

"That's not a very sanitary practice," Kat said from the next stall.

Latishia huffed. "Don't they have water treatment plants in this country?"

"Let's ask our tour guide about this. I wonder if we have to do this everywhere in Peru?" I said while righting my clothes.

We took turns washing up at the sinks.

Kat squirted sanitizer into our palms. "If we can't drink the water, I don't trust that soap and water will be sufficient for cleaning our hands."

We followed the jostling crowd to the baggage claim area and grabbed our luggage.

I grinned. "So far, so good. All our luggage made it."

We joined the line to go through customs and waited.

My heart rate accelerated as we drew closer to the customs officials. "Dear Lord, please don't let anything bad happen," I mumbled to myself. The way our luck had gone so far, any number of problems could crop up.

When it was my turn, I approached the customs officer, who was two inches shorter than me.

His brown eyes looked into mine and then scanned me like I might be carrying a weapon of mass destruction.

My meager breakfast did the cha cha inside my stomach.

In heavily accented English, he asked, "How long will you be in Peru?"

"One week," I answered, my throat dry from flying and anxiety.

His voice dropped an octave. "Why did you come to our country?"

I swallowed. "To see your beautiful ruins." I offered a shaky smile.

He flipped through my passport, found an empty page, eyed me once more, and stamped it. His expression remained the same when he handed it back to me. "Enjoy your vacation."

I hurried to join the Divas, who stood together waiting for me. "We made it through! We're in Lima, Peru."

"Where to now?" Latishia asked.

I shrugged, then pointed. "Follow everyone else."

When we approached the doors leading out of the airport, at least twenty people held signs. None of them said Peru Tourism. I walked closer and spotted a man holding a sign that said, "Incan Elite Tours." In his other hand, he held another one with our names on it.

Gina nudged me. "I thought we booked with Peru Tourism?"

"We did. Let's find out what's going on." I pulled my case over to the guy. "Hola. I'm Phoenix O'Leary. This is Gina Bongiorno, Latishia Snide, and Kat Wang."

"Hola! Welcome to Peru. I am José, I will take you to your hotel."

I gestured to include all the Divas. "We're confused. We booked through Peru Tourism, not Incan Elite."

José's white teeth gleamed in his tanned face. "Peru Tourism is our country's tourism booking agency, but they don't provide the actual tours. They assigned your complete tour to Incan Elite. We will make sure your needs are met."

My shoulders lowered with relief. "Good enough for me. We're sorry about our flight change and our delay getting off the plane." I explained the entire situation while he guided us out of the airport. I held up one hand to block the blinding sun while fumbling through my purse with the other for my sunglasses.

He stopped outside a small grocery. "Best to buy some water here. You must only drink filtered, bottled water."

Kat stepped forward. "It's my understanding that we should also brush our teeth and rinse our toothbrush with bottled water. Is that true?"

"Sí. It is also good to keep your mouth and eyes closed when showering."

The Divas exchanged worried glances. Loud conversations in Spanish surrounded us. It made me feel isolated and vulnerable.

I wondered aloud, "What's in this water that's so bad?"

Gina sidled closer and whispered, "I'm not sure I want to know."

I decided to buy a large bottle of water. That way, I could refill my drinking container as needed. The Divas did the same.

With the water issue settled, we rolled our luggage out to the parking lot. A white passenger van with Incan Elite Tours written on the side was parked nearby. A driver got out and opened a sliding door. It was spotless inside and out. Peppermints and a box of tissues were within reach.

Gina grabbed four mints and gave us each one. "My mouth feels like the inside of a litter box."

"If anyone should know, it's you," Latishia said, eyes twinkling with mischief.

Gina crossed her arms and pinned her with a nasty glare. "What does that mean?"

Latishia pasted an innocent look on her face. "You're the only one who's had cats."

The driver and José loaded our luggage into the rear, while we sanitized the van under Kat's watchful gaze.

Our guide hopped into the front passenger seat. The driver slid behind the steering wheel.

Kat leaned forward in her seat. "We noticed signs in the baño that said to put the toilet paper into the trash can. Do we do that everywhere?"

José turned in his seat before answering. "Sí."

Gina shoved a stray curl out of her face. "Even at the hotels? We're staying at a four-star hotel."

"Sí. The hotels are modern, but the sewer system is not."

Latishia crossed her arms, and her lower lip protruded.

I took a deep breath and released it, ready to relax and begin my vacation in Peru, despite the antiquated sewer system. I closed my eyes and thought about having a second cup of coffee.

The moment we left the airport parking lot, my eyes popped open, and my sense of peace evaporated like mist on a sunny day.

The traffic terrified me. It was vehicular pandemonium. I alternated between holding my breath and hyperventilating. There were lines painted on the pavement, like in America. The drivers treated their confines as mere suggestions, often riding for periods in two lanes. Blinkers blinked once before the vehicles whipped over to the next lane. Scooters darted between the bumpers of larger vehicles, seeming to dare the drivers to hit them. Horns honked warnings that were ignored.

A massive truck barreled by in front of us, missing the front bumper of our van by inches. "Sweet Baby Jesus," Latishia yelped.

Gina squeezed my arm, saying a Hail Mary under her breath. Kat, pale as a freshly laundered sheet, clutched the edges of her seat.

I kept trying to gulp air between my gasps of fear. I couldn't decide if it would be less stressful to close my eyes and hope for the best or keep them open and stomp the missing brake on the floorboard.

Our smiling guide explained the sights along the way in a calm tone, as if Armageddon wasn't occurring around us. He hitched his head to his right. "There is our beach."

Strange spiky fir trees dotted the shoulder of the road. I pointed at them and asked, "What are those?"

José looked where I pointed and replied, "Trees."

Tired, scared, and cranky, I rolled my eyes. "I can see they're trees. What kind?"

He shrugged. "Some kind of evergreen."

The beach and nearby ocean looked foggy. I wasn't sure if the effect came from fog or pollution. We seemed to be winding our way up a hill from the beach toward the city. The entire tall dirt cliff to our left looked like a landslide waiting to happen. We reached the top and drove through the older part of Lima, which was covered with graffiti. Twenty minutes later, in a posher section of the city, we pulled up to a modern-looking hotel.

"This is El Tambo, your hotel," José said as he and the driver exited the van.

The moment my feet hit the pavement, I felt the urge to kneel and hug it.

Gina stepped out and looked up, crossed herself, and said, "Thank you, God."

Latishia added a hearty, "Amen!"

Kat swayed for a moment when she left the van.

I reached out to steady her. "Are you all right?"

"I don't normally get this car sick, but that whole experience was a bit much. I do better if I sit in the front seat."

We left the muggy heat and entered the air-conditioned lobby of the hotel. We checked in, and a pot-bellied man carried our luggage up the stairs.

"A breakfast buffet is available in their dining room around the corner," José indicated with a wave. "It's included in your stay. I will be back at two o'clock to escort you on your city tour. Wear comfortable walking shoes, and don't forget your camera." He handed each of us an olive-green pouch with *PeruTourism.com* on the outside. "This is your entire itinerary for your trip." He gave a brief wave and left.

"I don't know about y'all, but I need coffee," I said, heading toward the buffet.

Gina pulled her abundant curls into a scrunchy. "The heck with coffee, I need a Xanax! My nerves are shot. I thought Naples, Italy, had crazy drivers."

A long gray granite countertop stretched along one wall. All the food items on it were labeled with white cards in Spanish and English. The long wooden cabinet underneath had open sections that held dinner plates, salad plates, bowls, cups, and saucers.

I grabbed a cup and placed it under the spout of a metal West Bend Coffee urn. The brew gushed dark and fragrant from the spout.

Gina looked over my shoulder. "That's pretty wicked looking. Pour half into my cup, and we'll have café con leche. There's a pump container over there that says hot milk."

Kat yawned. "At least they have hot water and tea bags."

Latishia stood across the room, rubbing her chin with a thumb and forefinger. "Did you notice these plaster Inca statues on the wall?"

I stepped back and looked up. Each of the four wore a different painted mask.

"Based on the genitalia, some are male and others female," I pointed out.

Gina glanced up. "They don't have much going on in the male department."

Kat giggled while she loaded her plate with scrambled eggs, toast, cut-up meats, cheeses, and fresh fruit.

We followed her example. After we completed our second breakfast, we lingered over our hot beverages and discussed our favorite topic—men.

"We've been so busy dashing through airports and dodging crazy drivers that we haven't had time to discuss your guys' reactions to our trip. I've already told you about Mike's."

Gina stirred her café con leche. "Chris was fine with it. He only asked that I text him when possible, so he knows I'm okay. I texted him on the way here, which wasn't easy with all the honking and lane changes."

"Don't forget the praying," I said.

Kat took off her glasses to wipe away the steam rising from her hot tea. "Same with Don. I guess things are different when it's a long-distance relationship. Since Don's still in Fort Walton Beach, most of our contact is through texts and FaceTime anyway."

Latishia pushed back from the table and stretched. "Things are different when your man lives in the same city. Aaron wasn't a bit happy about this trip. The way he carried on, you'd have thought I was leaving for a year, not a week. We had words when he dropped me off at the airport in Huntsville. That's why I was late, not that it mattered. He said I chose the Divas over him."

"What?" I put down my cup. "What's with these guys? I didn't know it was a competition."

Gina snorted and threw her hands in the air. "If it wasn't for a Diva vacation, you would've never met him."

"True," I agreed.

"I swear, the man thinks I'm puttin' him off," Latishia said. She picked up her cup and downed the rest of her coffee.

"Are you?" Kat asked, replacing her glasses.

Latishia hesitated. "Maybe."

"What's the deal?" I asked as I picked up my water bottle.

"I don't think Dante's ready yet. He needs some time to adjust to things."

I eyed her. "I think you need some space to figure this out. Do you feel like you're betraying Lamar?"

Latishia's first husband was shot during a convenience store robbery while Dante was an infant.

She shook her head. "I think it's more about Dante. My next-door neighbor, Teesh, ended up divorced because her man couldn't get along with her kids."

Gina stabbed a slice of porchetta and eyed it. "Believe me, I've seen plenty of busted marriages because the kids waged guerilla warfare on a stepparent. You're right to give Aaron and Dante some time to settle things."

Latishia nodded. "That's what this vacation is all about. We need to distance ourselves from our daily lives and the men in them. We all need a new perspective. Mama's always said, 'Men muck up a woman's perspective about life.'" She put down her fork and wiped her mouth and hands. "Phoenix, you told us about Mike. How did Brent react?"

"I found the difference between Mike and Brent's reactions to be interesting. Brent was worried for my safety. He admitted he'd miss me and asked me to text him daily so he'd know I was safe." I gripped my mug. "I still can't believe Mike got so bent out of shape about this trip. He acted like I was searching for a new man or something."

Gina chuckled and fluttered her lashes. "You did find Mike on our last vacation."

I lowered my voice and leaned forward. "I don't know if you've noticed or not, but I haven't seen a native taller than five-foot-five. I'm not used to being taller than most of the males. I prefer tall men. I don't think Mike has anything to worry about."

"That's true, but they all have luscious thick dark hair," Gina said.

After our discussion, we all piled into the tiny elevator and rode to the third floor. We agreed to meet in the lobby in thirty minutes.

I liked my room. Unlike some European hotel rooms, this one had a king-sized bed, a desk, and a spotless bathroom. A small sign told guests to not flush tissue down the toilet. I shrugged. "When in Peru…." I inspected the mattress to make sure there were no bed bugs. Pleased to find no pests, I decided to brush my teeth, reminding myself to use bottled water.

***

At the agreed-upon time, Gina, Kat, and I met downstairs near the door.

Kat pushed up her glasses. "Where's Latishia?"

The elevator door opened, and out popped Latishia. When she joined us, she seemed out of breath. "I forgot my water bottle. I had to rush back and get it."

Gina pulled the packet of information from her purse. "Did anyone notice our guide is picking us up tomorrow at five in the morning to take us to the airport?"

"You're kidding." Latishia said, fishing through her large bag for her copy.

"I wonder why it's so early? Our flight doesn't leave until eight," I said.

Kat shrugged. "Maybe he's trying to beat the traffic?"

We left the hotel and ventured out onto the streets of Lima. The heat wrapped around me like a damp blanket. We passed two guys playing music. One banged on a small drum held between his thighs, and the other played the accordion.

When we were out of earshot, I said, "I wish we could transplant all the Peruvian men's thick, shiny hair onto the heads of the bald guys in America. We'd make a fortune."

Kat looked over her shoulder and chuckled. "Good idea."

We passed a fountain, sidewalk cafes, and stores with apartments on the upper floors. This area of town was neat, clean, and graffiti-free, but I hadn't forgotten the many areas we'd passed that looked poor and shabby.

After an hour of wandering around, we decided to eat lunch at a sidewalk café on a pedestrian-only street. Café de la Paz looked inviting, with its copper-colored umbrellas and pots of greenery that screened its patrons from people strolling past. I decided to try a chicken, ham, spinach, and mozzarella cheese crepe listed in the menu as "De Pollo y Mozzarella Gratinada."

Kat wiped her glasses and placed them back on her nose. "This is the first chance I've had to relax since we left home."

Gina unwrapped her eating utensils. "I agree, it's been hectic. This place is quaint and is a perfect shady spot."

"I'm happy we made it to Lima in time to go on our tour this afternoon. Nothing gripes me more than to prepay for something and not get to go," I said.

Our food arrived, and the Divas did what we do best—eat.

I ate every morsel of my delicious crepe while immersed in the sights and sounds of the city.

We asked for our checks, and our waitress soon returned. I looked at the total and gasped. "Twenty-four soles!"

Gina stared at hers. "I had the salmon crepe, so mine is twenty-six soles."

Latishia glared at me. "I thought this would be a cheap trip."

I raised my hand. "Wait, I forgot about the exchange rate." I did the calculations on my phone. "Mine's only eight dollars, American."

My friends all exhaled their relief. We paid and wandered back to the hotel so we could shower and grab a quick nap before our tour.

CHAPTER 8: The First Tour

At two o'clock, José popped into the hotel lobby. "Oh, good. You are all here." He held the door open for us to exit.

The minute we left the lobby and entered the humid street, Kat's glasses fogged. Traffic noise and honking horns vibrated through the exhaust-laden air.

A small blue and white tour bus, with four people peering out the window, waited at the curb. It blocked part of the two-lane street.

José gestured toward the vehicle. "We must stop at two more hotels to pick up the rest of the tourists."

The smiling driver opened the door, and we stepped up into the frigid coach. We each claimed a window seat. I was the only one who'd brought a camera other than an iPhone. After Kat reminded us, we each wiped down all the surfaces we might touch. I suspected the Divas would need group therapy for obsessive-compulsive tendencies after returning home. Some of the Spanish-speaking tourists pointed and chuckled before conversing among themselves.

The bus stopped at two more hotels. We had twelve people on the tour, plus a driver, and English- and Spanish-speaking tour guides. The Spanish-speaking guide shooed his group toward the rear of the bus. José waved for the English speakers to move forward. He smiled and gestured out the window. "Welcome to Lima, The City of Kings."

Our first stop was a 1200-year-old pre-Inca construction called Huaca Huallamarca. I climbed out and looked up at the immense structure, which looked like a flattened pyramid made of millions of beige mud bricks.

Kat shaded her eyes as she looked up. "Do we get to go inside?"

"No," José said. "You can come back on your own if you like. The museum fee is sixty-five dollars, and this site alone would take three hours to tour. That is why we see only the outside."

We were leaving Lima in the morning. The Divas gave a collective sigh.

We whizzed past different sights. José pointed to his left. "There is the Magical Fountain Circuit located in the Parque de la Reserva. It is nineteen acres and has thirteen first-class water fountains."

I craned my neck, but only caught a glimpse of water between the bushes as we sped past.

We pulled into a parking slot at the main square.

Kat waved us away from a member of the Spanish-speaking group. "That guy keeps coughing. Stay as far away from him as possible. It may only be allergies, but I don't want to catch a cold and be miserable for the rest of our trip."

"Me, either," Gina said, giving him an icy look.

"Until we get off this tour, we wipe down the seats every time we return to the bus. Thank Buddha he's sitting in the back, and we're in the front." She reached into her purse and pulled out a small bottle of Purell hand sanitizer. "Try not to touch your faces until you're sanitized." She squirted a little blob into each of our hands.

José stepped out of the vehicle and swept his arm in an arc. "Is it not beautiful?" He pointed toward a building. "See where the soldiers stand guard on each side of the door. It is the Government Palace, the official home of Martín Vizcarra, the president of Peru." He beamed with pride.

Latishia squinted at the soldiers behind the tall wrought iron fence before putting on her sunglasses. "They look like Alabama fans to me."

I took a closer look at the soldiers' uniforms and saw what she meant. They wore red pants tucked into black boots, topped by white tunic shirts with large red epaulets on the shoulders. The guards wore shiny gold helmets with long, black braided hair-like tails that fell down their backs.

Latishia pursed her lips and added, "Well, maybe not those helmets with the horse tails hanging down. Can you imagine Alabama football players trying to make a touchdown wearing those helmets? An opponent could grab that braid of hair and whip 'em around." She illustrated with a gesture that looked more like wringing the neck of a chicken.

Gina laughed. "The officials would have to invent a new type of personal foul. They could call it, hair-yanking."

Latishia snickered. "I prefer tail-grabbing."

Kat wagged her finger. "Girl, if Mama Snide heard you say that, you'd be in trouble for sure."

Ignoring the banter, I shaded my eyes from the bright sun. "The palace looks huge. Do we get to go inside?"

José shook his head. "Not enough time. The facade of the palace is a neo-Baroque style with a Neoclassical side facade. I'm sorry to tell you we missed the changing of the guard. That happened at noon." He gestured for us to follow. "Come see the Basilica Cathedral of Lima. It is stunning." He walked across the square with us in tow. He turned to face us walking backward and said, "Construction began in 1535, but it wasn't completed until 1649."

Gina rubbed her hands together. "Now we're talking! Nothing like a good old Catholic Cathedral. Is it dedicated to a saint?"

José grinned. "Saint John the Apostle. It is unique because the architect, Francisco Becerra, constructed it using the Gothic, Renaissance, and Neoclassical architectural styles."

Kat shook her head. "And they say women can't make up their minds."

Gina crossed her arms. "Just because you're a Buddhist, it doesn't give you permission to make fun of the cathedral."

Kat walked over and put her arm around Gina's waist. "I'm not making fun of the church. You know me better than that, don't you? I was making fun of the indecisive architect."

Gina nodded and returned the hug. "Maybe he just wanted it all."

Kat chuckled. "Just like a man."

"I like the symmetry of the two bell towers. It gives the structure balance," I said. "Do we get to go inside?"

José shifted from one foot to another. "Uh, no."

"The heck with that!" Gina took off in a speed walk, arms swinging.

The Divas hustled behind her with José trailing in our wake. When I looked back, the rest of the English-speaking part of our group stood rooted to the spot for several seconds before following.

I paused inside for a moment to appreciate the checkerboard of large black and white tiles covering the floor. The gold-covered wooden arches were accented by special lighting. Individual chairs were set in rows to create a long center aisle that led to the altar.

Gina led us deeper into the church. I counted fourteen side chapels before we arrived at the elaborate wooden choir stalls.

Latishia leaned closer and peered at a carving. "Who are all these folks carved on here? We don't have stuff like this in a Baptist church."

José touched one of the carvings. "They are virgins, apostles, and saints."

My attention was glued to the gold-plated two-level altar that stood at the rear.

"Beautiful," Kat said.

"I've seen prettier," Gina said. "Someday we'll go to Venice or Rome. Y'all will be amazed."

José stepped forward. "As I said, the original church was completed in 1538, but it had several renovations done in the 17th century due to earthquake damage."

"Earthquakes?" Latishia gave him a wide-eyed look before glancing around.

José nodded. "We have many earthquakes in Peru."

After the group left the basilica, they drifted toward the multi-tiered black cast-iron fountain. José pointed at the angel blowing a horn on the top. "This is the only colonial architectural element that has survived. It was dedicated in 1651."

I gazed up at the angel. "I'd love to have this water feature in my yard. You know how much I like angels."

José waved to get our attention. "Next, we see the Archbishop's Palace. Its facade is the Neocolonial architectural style."

Gina tapped her chin with an index finger. "Those porches look like something I've seen in Venice."

"What kind of wood is it?" asked Kat.

"The balconies are carved from cedar," José said.

"Beautiful workmanship," I said as I wondered what it would be like to sit on one of them.

Latishia frowned. "I'm bettin' we don't get to go in there, either."

José's downcast expression said it all.

Latishia's lower lip protruded. "This tour reminds me of window shopping."

Gina looked displeased. "Reminds me of a meal with hors d'oeuvres and no entrée."

José started walking. "Next, we see the Municipal Palace. It is like your city halls."

The sprawling building was painted mustard yellow with white trim. For once, José ushered us into a long hall covered with paintings. Afterward, we were hustled into the bus and taken down toward the beach.

We left the bus at a beautiful park that overlooked the ocean. A large sculpture of a canoodling older couple dominated the area.

José said, "This is El Beso, The Kiss. It was carved by one of our famous artists, Victor Delfín."

The beige statue of a reclining woman embraced and kissed by a man showed romance wasn't only for the young and svelte. People circled it, pointing and snapping photos. The salt breeze ruffled my hair, while the sun warmed my face.

Latishia smiled. "I like it."

Gina shrugged. "Makes me feel like an ant-sized voyeur."

"Come." José herded us toward the bus.

Once onboard, I asked, "Is the chocolate place next?"

José looked at his watch and frowned. "No, the Chocolate Museum is not on your tour."

I pulled out my paperwork from Peru Tourism. "It says right here that we will go to the Chocolate Museum." I thrust the paper toward him and pointed at the correct section.

He squinted at the schedule and shook his head. "No time."

I snatched the schedule from his grasp and gave him my meanest stink-eye. "It's not good to come between a woman and her chocolate."

"Amen to that, sister," said Latishia, her lower lip protruding even more.

Gina glowered from her seat. "I'm reporting this to Peru Tourism."

José's jaw tightened. "We have no time for chocolates. The traffic will be bad."

With a lilting tone, Kat said, "Karma."

Traffic was already horrible. I failed to see how a delay could make it any worse. *I wonder if he's punishing us for going inside the cathedral?*

A traffic circle during a Lima traffic jam was a gut-wrenching, heart-pounding experience. At that moment, it looked more like a parking lot than a traffic circle. The cars barely moved. Our driver and tour guide rolled down their windows and pulled the side-view mirrors in, so the bus could squeeze between two cars. I held my breath until we made it past. My jaw didn't unclench until our tour bus stopped in front of our hotel.

Once we were safe inside the air-conditioned lobby, Kat said, "I'm so glad we're off that bus. The guy in back sounded like he was hacking his lungs out by the time we got off."

I turned and said, "Me, too. I don't care where we eat as long as we walk there. I'm not riding a cab in this city."

CHAPTER 9: Shake and Rattle

I rode the elevator down to the lobby at a quarter till five the next morning. It was dark. The two people who worked nights slept on two of the lobby couches.

Unsure what to do, I cleared my throat.

No one moved.

I bellowed, "Good morning."

They sprang up, looking startled. The guy blinked while running his hands through his disheveled hair.

The woman stood and adjusted her clothes before rushing behind the front desk counter. Seconds later, the man turned on the lobby lights.

"I understand breakfast is included with my stay. I was hoping to grab a quick bite before heading to the airport," I said, feeling a bit sheepish.

The male clerk glanced at his watch. "Sí, but it won't be available until six."

The elevator door opened and Kat exited with her backpack slung on one shoulder. She rolled her suitcase over to me.

"Bad news. Breakfast won't be available until six," I told her.

The female clerk spoke up. "I can make a quick pot of coffee." She pointed to a small coffee station against the opposite wall of the lobby.

"That would be great," Kat said. "Can you manage some hot water for tea?"

"Sí." The clerk hurried across the lobby and began the process.

Kat fished a couple of protein bars out of her backpack and handed one to me.

"Thanks," I said, unwrapping mine.

We'd finished our protein bars and were sipping our second cups of coffee and tea when Gina and Latishia arrived.

"Coffee!" Gina's face brightened. "Where?"

I pointed toward the coffee station.

"I'm right behind you," said Latishia, leaving her suitcase and backpack near one of the gray couches.

When they joined us on the sofas, I said, "Breakfast isn't until six."

"Bummer," Latishia said.

Kat handed each of them a protein bar.

Gina tore open the wrapper. "You're so smart. Why didn't I think to bring some of these?" She broke off a chunk, popped it into her mouth, and chewed.

Latishia sat down and opened hers. Her blouse of different shades of green looked like a tropical forest. "She's right. We need to buy some more of these just in case. I'll buy the next round."

I chuckled. "Sounds like you're talking about drinks, not protein bars."

We finished the remainder of our meager breakfast in silence. We were trashing the wrappers when the van pulled up outside.

José jumped out and pushed open the door. "Hola! Good, you are ready. Please roll your bags to the rear of the van."

We thanked the hotel staff and walked out into the dark, humid morning. Halos formed around the streetlights, giving the scene a surreal effect. Nothing stirred.

The driver, whose name I didn't catch, loaded our luggage while José helped us into the spotless van. We sanitized anyway. I wondered if José thought we were all germophobes. We drove away unnoticed by the rest of the slumbering hotel guests. Everyone was silent as we passed the dark windows of businesses not yet open. It had rained overnight, and the streets looked like polished glass. It was a Lima I'd never seen before and would probably never see again.

Gina yawned and then gave me a wicked wink. "It's a shame we missed the Chocolate Museum yesterday. I could use some dark chocolate about now."

I nudged her with my foot and gave her one of my famous *let it go* looks.

Our guide and driver exchanged displeased looks and exchanged a brief conversation in Spanish. They nodded to each other. The driver veered off onto a backstreet. It was a steep, winding, two-lane cobblestone road. The vibration made me grateful I'd made a pit stop before we left.

"Sweet Baby Jesus! This road is going to scramble my internal organs like eggs in a blender," Latishia said as she held her girls. "I need a better bra for this road."

"It's rough," I said, holding my stomach. My coffee and power bar felt like they were being agitated by a rogue washing machine.

"Merda," was all Gina managed to say. Her tight mouth spoke volumes.

"We will be off this road soon," José said, his white teeth glowing in the blue light from the van's dashboard. I didn't like the glint in his eye when he chuckled. "We thought you'd like a different view on the way out of town."

"What view? It's dark and everyone else is still asleep," I said.

Ten minutes later, the van hit smoother pavement. The Divas exchanged relieved looks, especially Kat, who looked ready to spew her guts. I prayed she'd get it under control and soon. When the van arrived at the airport, the driver unloaded our luggage while a smug-looking José helped us out. He winked at the driver and grinned.

Kat was the last one out. José held on to her, trying to keep her from toppling over. She took off her glasses and ran her hand over her sweating face. "Car sick."

She bent and vomited on José's shoes.

He swore and leaped back into the driver, who landed on his backside.

Stench filled the air. My bile rose in empathy, causing me to swallow in self-defense. I suspected it was a combination of motion sickness and a hot flash that caused Kat to get sick.

"Oohwee!" Latishia backed away, waving her hand in front of her face.

Gina pulled a hand wipe from her purse and handed it to a pale Kat, who leaned against the van clutching her stomach.

"So sorry," Kat said, wiping her sweating face with the cloth.

Gina fanned her with a magazine that she'd tucked into her purse. Glaring at José, she said, "It's your fault for choosing such a bumpy road."

He had the decency to swap a guilty look with the driver while he pulled off his shoes.

Kat closed her eyes, took a few deep breaths, and put on her glasses. "I'm ready."

We followed José, who now wore only his socks, across the wet pavement and into the airport. It was busy for such an early hour. His wet socks left a trail of damp footprints across the floor.

He gave us our tickets to Cusco. "A guide from Incan Elite will meet you in Cusco. Look for the Incan Elite sign."

He made sure our luggage was checked in and left us at security, before rushing out in his stocking feet. Considering Kat's state, I thanked Saint Christopher that security was a breeze compared to the U.S.

I looked at Gina. "You still plan to report José for cutting our tour short?"

Gina rolled her eyes. "What do you think? Like you said yesterday, don't come between a woman and her chocolate. After that little fiasco on the cobblestone road, I'm definitely reporting him."

Kat blushed pink. "That was so embarrassing."

Gina raised her chin. "He deserved it. I think they took that road intentionally because he knew I planned to report him. Think of it as Karma."

"Lordy, I need a ladies' room," Latishia said. "My bladder has been jostled like an overfilled water balloon."

We all rushed to the nearest ladies' room and disposed of the tissue into the trashcan beside the toilet, as the signs directed.

We were happy to see we were seated together when we entered the plane. After disinfecting everything in sight, we settled down.

Kat pulled a bottle of pills from her bag. "Dr. Howard gave me prescriptions for several things we might need for this trip. He was concerned we might have problems with high altitude sickness since Huntsville's a mere six hundred feet above sea level." She shook the bottle. "Cusco is over eleven thousand feet above sea level. It will be one of the highest elevations we'll encounter. We need to take one of these pills now, so we don't have problems with high altitude sickness after we land. Sacred Valley, where we're going next, is only around nine thousand feet above sea level, so our time there will give our bodies a chance to acclimate." She handed out the pills.

"What's high altitude sickness?" I asked, eyeing the tablet in my hand.

"It happens when your body doesn't get enough oxygen. The symptoms are headache, nausea, and shortness of breath, especially after exercising," Kat swallowed her pill with a swig from her bottled water. "It can be lethal if the person has heart or breathing problems."

Gina held up her pill between two fingers. "Always travel with a nurse. Kat knows all and thinks of everything. Thanks to you and Dr. Howard."

Latishia and I agreed.

Kat grinned. "I'll tell him when I go back to work."

We landed in Cusco with no luggage issues or heart attack victims. I grabbed my backpack and thought, *What a relief.*

After we retrieved our luggage, we soon spotted our next guide. He stood about five-foot six with a small gut and a headful of straight dark hair. He looked to be in his early thirties.

Gina got to him first. "I think you're our Incan Elite guide."

After checking our documents, he placed his hand over his heart. "My name is André."

We all introduced ourselves. André led us to another spotless van. The driver loaded our luggage while we climbed inside.

André cocked his head while he watched us sanitize. "The van is clean."

Kat smiled and nodded. "Yes, it is, but now it's sanitized."

André glanced back at the driver loading our baggage and shrugged. "We will make a few stops before we take you to the Aranwa Hotel and Spas. First, we will stop at Racchi for a beautiful view." He handed us bottles of cold water. "Drink, please. Planes dehydrate you, and it is important to stay hydrated in higher altitudes."

Cusco was hilly. We passed what appeared to be a street market. Trucks of all shapes and sizes lined both sides of the street. A few appeared newer, but most looked well-used, with peeling paint and spots of rust. Blue tarps covered most of them, providing some shade for the vegetables. Bright red tomatoes contrasted against purple cabbage and several varieties of potatoes. I only recognized bananas among the multiple varieties of vibrantly colored fruit.

"The corn," I pointed. "It's huge. I've never seen kernels so large."

"The Incas experimented with corn crops for years. This is one of many varieties. They were famous for corn, potatoes, and cacao. We have some of the most flavorful potatoes in the world," André said. "Later you will see their laboratory."

Eyes wide with surprise, Latishia looked at me and mouthed, *The Incas had laboratories?*

I shrugged and looked out the window. A young mother, with a toddler secured to her back by a colorful blanket, ambled past. Older, plump women wore impressive black masculine-looking hats, long full skirts, and colorful shawls. Their braided hair hung in pigtails down their backs.

"Do the hats mean anything?" Latishia asked. "There seem to be several different types."

"Each district has a distinctive hat. This is a market day, so many people come to Cusco to buy," André said.

We passed a three-story building. The white letters on its large red sign spelled *Pollería*.

"What does that store sell?" Kat asked while snapping a photo on her phone.

"It is the poultry store."

After we left Cusco, the landscape became greener and more rural. Mountains rose on each side. We were now traveling through the Sacred Valley.

When we arrived at the Racchi viewpoint, the scenery didn't disappoint.

"Wow. I wish Aaron could see this. He loves this type of terrain," Latishia said.

"Oh, are you missing him already?" Gina asked with a sly grin.

Latishia crossed her arms. "Don't y'all miss your guys?"

Kat said, "I can't speak for Gina, but I miss Don all the time because of the long-distance situation."

They all turned to look at me. "I, well…"

"Uh, oh," Latishia said. "Don't you miss Mike and Brent a little bit?"

"Of course I do. It's, um, complicated." Desperate to change the subject, I turned to André. "Those mountains look like they popped straight out of the ground."

He nodded. "The deep ridges you see are caused by years of erosion. The town down in the valley is Racchi."

Latishia pointed. "There's a football field down there."

"Yes, Racchi is more modern and even has electricity. Many of the communities don't."

We exchanged shocked looks.

A breeze blew tendrils of hair across my face. I brushed them away and said, "I didn't realize electricity wasn't readily available."

"Many of Peru's smaller communities are remote," André said.

Latishia frowned. "Will they have electricity where we're going?"

"Sí. It is a tourist hotel."

Thirty minutes on two-lane roads brought us to our second stop. We left the van and followed André. Fields of waving green native grasses surrounded us. The sky was the color of a blue topaz. I threw my arms wide and inhaled a deep breath of clean mountain air.

"This is Moray," André said. "It was the Incas' botanical laboratory where they tried different crops. They may have done some of the first cross pollination."

We stared down into colossal round holes dug down in multiple terraces, with a cleared green circle of grass at the bottom of each one.

Kat adjusted her glasses. "Why did they dig down like that? Couldn't they just plant rows of plants?"

"Each level has different climate conditions," André said.

Latishia shook her head. A look of wonder crossed her face. "Those Incas thought of everything."

"Wait until you see Machu Picchu," said André. "You will be impressed."

Kat leaned further across the rope. "Why can't we get closer?"

He gestured with a wide arc of his hand. "Moray is a UNESCO World Heritage protected site. That is why it is roped off. We have many tourists and not all are considerate."

After seeing everything and taking individual and group photos, we returned to the van.

"I wonder how long it took the Incas to dig all those deep terraced holes?" Gina asked.

"Who knows." Kat blew a stray hair out of her face. "I'm curious as to why the Incas dug circles and not squares or rectangles? When I get back home, I'm going to have Jack research all of this. He has an assignment coming up and was wondering what to write about. He can use some of my photos."

We drove through miles of beautiful scenery. Mountains rose on each side of us. With every mile, I found my tension leaving. I spotted a town ahead.

I leaned forward. "What's the name of this little town?"

"Urubamba," André said.

Gina pointed out the window. "Why do they have all these triangle banners strung across the street? They use flags like these at used car lots at home."

André turned to face us with a merry grin. "Tomorrow is Carnival. Booths will be set up on the soccer field. Everyone in town will attend and celebrate."

We saw more women dressed in traditional dress. Their hats looked slightly different from the ones we saw in Cusco.

We drove off the main road onto a small paved one that ran along a cornfield.

"We are here," André said, giving us another wide grin. "Aranwa Hotel and Spas."

CHAPTER 10: The Text

The gate of the Aranwa Hotel and Spas was unique, but I wouldn't describe it as beautiful. Two large block towers, one twice as tall as the other, supported a narrow Spanish tile roof. The large wooden doors were open. Gravel popped under the tires when the van pulled into a small circular courtyard. Verdant tropical vegetation lined the courtyard and emphasized a flat round fountain shooting water into the air.

Latishia exited first. She stretched and walked over to examine some of the plants.

The moment I stepped out, I heard and smelled river water. "Is there a river close by?"

André pointed toward a wall. "Behind the hotel. There is a way for you to walk beside it."

"What's the name of the river?" I asked.

Gina rolled her eyes with the verve of an adolescent. "What is it with you and rivers?" She turned to André. "Ever since I've known her, she's had a river fascination."

"The Vilcanota," André answered.

Latishia fingered a large green leaf. "It's so lush around here. Mama would love to have some of these plants in her yard."

Gina joined her. "We're near the equator, so tropical vegetation grows well around here. I'm not sure if any of these would survive a freeze in North Alabama."

We followed our guide through the front doors of the hotel. We stopped, transfixed by a large floor-to-ceiling stained glass window that depicted a stylized image of sunrise over the local mountains. The highest peak reminded me of photos of Machu Picchu. The sun shining through the window painted the pale floor of the spacious lobby yellow, orange, red, turquoise, blue, and purple. It brought to mind a watercolor painting I once saw on display in a gallery.

I fumbled for my camera and began taking shots. "So beautiful. I've never seen so much orange used in a window."

Gina nodded. "I'm impressed. They don't have windows that tall and wide in many of the churches I've seen."

André herded us toward the check-in counter.

The female clerk smiled. "Hola. Welcome to Aranwa Hotel and Spas. Please sign in. Your room is prepaid, and breakfast is included. We will need a credit card to cover any additional expenses."

Once the Divas had signed in and settled the business end of our stay, the clerk pointed at two men. "These gentlemen will escort you to your rooms in the colonial section."

The men rolled our suitcases toward a door, and we followed. The minute we stepped outside, we halted again so we could admire the landscaping.

Latishia sighed, placing a hand over her heart. "Mama would love to see this."

I took a deep breath and enjoyed the scent of flowers. The whole area was a marvel. A small stream with a waterfall ran through the property. On a nearby knoll, llamas and alpacas were staked on the grass to graze. We followed the two men across a bridge. A peacock strutted along an adjacent path and squawked a greeting.

Kat cringed. "For beautiful birds, they have such an abrasive song."

Gina shaded her eyes with her hand and pointed. "Look, they have a church. I bet they do weddings here."

We all stopped to admire the small chapel.

"I want to check it out later," Gina said.

Unable to resist, I imitated one of her eye rolls. "Girl, what is it with you and churches?"

Gina cocked a hip and crossed her arms. "I'm Catholic, remember?" She winked at Latishia. "You and Aaron can come back someday soon, be married, and honeymoon at the hotel."

Latishia did her neck thing. "Don't you start pushing me toward matrimony. What do you know about it anyway? You've never been married."

Gina waved her hand in dismissal. "Enough to avoid it."

"Now, ladies." I held up both hands. "We're on vacation. I personally want to forget about the men in my life for a bit longer, so I can gain some much-needed perspective."

We continued along a landscaped path until we entered a courtyard with a fountain. The edges were surrounded by small trees, tables with umbrellas, and stone benches. Upon further inspection, I found the fountain was unlike any I'd ever seen.

Latishia cocked her head and squinted. "Is that a giant ear of corn on top spouting water?"

Kat pushed her glasses back into place before moving closer. "Looks like it. The Incas seemed to be interested in corn as one of their main crops. The faces spouting water out of their mouths further down look Incan."

"Welcome to the land of the Inca," I said, whirling. "I'd love to have this set up in my back yard."

"So would I," Gina said, "But with a different fountain."

Grinning, Latishia asked, "You don't like corn?"

Gina flipped her hair over a shoulder. "I'm a cherub girl, myself."

We followed the porters up some steps. I stopped on the landing and looked up. A large brass crystal chandelier with several layers of teardrop pendants hung over the landing in the open stairwell. "Just when I think I've seen it all."

Latishia looked up. "Strange place to put such a fancy chandelier."

The porters explained in broken English that breakfast was served in the main restaurant, lunch was served in the bar, and the evening meal was available in both locations. After making plans to meet for lunch, we parted ways to unpack and check out our accommodations.

When I entered my room, I discovered it was a suite. *Wow. I can't believe this.* In the first large room, cream and tan walls rose high to a whitewashed A-frame ceiling. There was a sizable, elaborate writing table surrounded by four ornately carved chairs in the center of the room. It looked so valuable, I was afraid to set my purse on the tooled leather top. *This looks like an antique, and the paintings and sculptures look original and expensive.* Another impressive traditional crystal chandelier hung over the desk. I shook my head. *They sure do love their fancy light fixtures.*

I rolled my suitcase into the next room. It held a king-size bed dominated by a golden carved headboard with a backing of red velvet, complete with one of Gina's beloved cherubs. The side tables matched the headboard and were attached to the wall. There was a small matching writer's desk against the wall across from the bed. *You don't see a headboard like that every day.* I glanced up and spotted an even more glamorous crystal chandelier, whose layers of clear prisms created small patches of rainbows on the walls and ceiling.

Curious to discover if there would be some sort of prismed light fixture dangling over the tub, I peeked into the bathroom. Shiny black stone covered the floors and walls, creating an ultra-modern, cave-like effect. The large vanity had a white marble countertop. The glassed-in shower was generous, and the pristine white hydro tub could hold two people sitting side-by-side. Naughty thoughts about that tub raced through my head.

I wandered back into the bedroom and sat on the bed. *It's hard to believe this luxury hotel exists in a rural area where many people are poor, undereducated, and don't have electricity. I'm so blessed.*

Thirty minutes later, the Divas met in the bar for lunch. Once seated, we compared rooms. Each of us had a suite, but the specific decorations varied, unlike the cookie-cutter décor of many hotels in the States.

I pointed at the menu. "Oh look, guinea pig is one of the options."

The waiter smiled. "It is a delicacy in our country."

Latishia lowered her menu and glared across the table. "Phoenix Dixie O'Leary! Are you going to eat a helpless, cuddly animal? Didn't you have a guinea pig as a pet?"

Gina nudged me and smirked. "You're in trouble again. She used your full name."

I raised my chin. "For your information, I had a hamster named Clarabell, not a guinea pig. If you knew anything about guinea pigs, you'd know they aren't cuddly." I turned to the waiter. "Is it served whole?"

He shook his head. "The flesh is removed and then cooked."

Relieved to hear this, I tapped the listed item. "In that case, I'll have the guinea pig, please."

Latishia pushed out her lower lip and shot a disapproving look my way.

Kat closed her menu. With a slight upturn of her lips, she said, "I'll try it, too."

Latishia shook her head and mumbled, "The Chinese will eat anything."

Kat glared across the table at Latishia. "This from a woman who eats hog jowl on New Year's Day."

Latishia raised her bosom to its full splendor. "It's for good luck."

The waiter beamed, eying her ample assets. "Guinea pig is also good luck."

Latisha harrumphed again and raised her menu.

Gina winked at Kat and me. "I'll have the same."

The three of us stared at Latishia, who lowered her menu.

Unfazed, she ordered the alpaca steak.

Gina pointed at the three animals staked on the lawn grazing. "What? You're going to eat one of those sweet animals on the lawn?"

Latishia waved a dismissive hand. "I'm sure it's not one of them. Besides, those are probably llamas," Latishia said.

"Maybe," I conceded. "For all you know, it could be one of their siblings or cousins."

Latishia tightened her jaw. "Stop giving me grief! At least I'm not eating a sweet fluffy guinea pig."

We sat silent until our glasses of wine arrived.

I took a sip and let the fruity flavor of the Chardonnay flow over my taste buds. Taking a deep breath, I released it and relaxed into my seat. *This is more like it. Peace of mind at last.*

My phone pinged with a text.

I dug it out of my purse, hoping everything was all right at home. Shocked, I stared at the phone. "Oh, crap!"

"What?" Gina asked. "Is Buffy okay?"

I grimaced. "She's fine, I guess. No news is good news, right? It's a text from Brent."

Kat leaned forward, concern clouding her face. "Did his father have another heart attack?"

I shook my head. "Nothing like that."

Latishia huffed and crossed her arms. "What then? Are you gonna make us wait all day?"

My hand trembled a bit. "He's been promoted."

Kat removed her glasses and wiped them with her cloth napkin. "That's good news, isn't it?"

I looked up. "The promotion means he's being transferred next month." My gut felt tight.

Gina sat straighter. "Where?"

"He didn't say."

The phone pinged again.

My shoulders slumped. "Good grief, Brent's moving to Seattle."

Gina set down her glass of merlot. "Seattle! That's clear across the country."

Latishia raised her wine glass in a toast. "To Brent's promotion. Phoenix, it seems Brent's employer has solved your problem of dealing with two beaux."

The phone pinged once again.

I read the next text, and my stomach flipped. I looked up. "Not really. He wants me to move to Seattle with him."

Gina's jaw dropped. "He expects you to drop everything and move to the West Coast?"

CHAPTER 11: The Discussion

Gina scowled. "What does that mean exactly? Is Brent proposing marriage, or is he expecting you to move in and play house?"

I shrugged as the waiter arrived, putting a temporary end to the subject. He set a well-presented dish of guinea pig with fresh vegetables in front of me. "It smells delicious."

Latishia looked down her nose. "Poor baby animal."

The waiter reached over and placed Latishia's alpaca steak in front of her.

Grinning, Kat said, "Move that plate further to the left, Latishia."

Latishia's brow scrunched. She looked at the plate, then Kat. "Why?"

Kat placed the napkin into her lap. "You don't want those lovely animals on the lawn to see you eat their cousin."

Gina erupted into giggles. "Stop, you two. I can't eat and laugh at the same time." She cut off a section of the guinea pig and placed it in her mouth. "Oh, my! This is delicious."

Kat nodded. "I agree."

The waiter beamed. "Is everything to your satisfaction?"

We all nodded, so he left.

"What does it taste like?" Latishia leaned closer to look at Kat's plate.

"It's not like anything else I've ever eaten, but it's delicious," I said.

Latishia nudged Gina with her elbow. "Oh, heck. Give me a bite."

Gina placed a small slice on her plate. We all stopped eating to better see her reaction.

Latishia eyed it ruefully before placing it into her mouth. She chewed. "I must admit it's quite tasty. Even better than the alpaca, which is excellent."

"Now that we've settled the guinea pig debate and the waiter has left, what do you plan to do about Brent?" Kat asked.

Latishia forked a bite of her steak. "I think the first thing Phoenix needs to decide is if she loves Brent or Mike. If she loves Mike, the whole Brent issue is moot."

All three of them paused to look at me.

"That's the problem. I love both men for different reasons."

Gina nodded. "I can see how that could happen. It does complicate the matter."

Kat paused before taking another bite. "Which one do you love the most?"

"I'm not sure. Neither guy is quite my forever man. They aren't a perfect fit." I shrugged. "Then again, is any man?"

Latishia did her neck thing. "Leave it to a psychologist to complicate the situation."

We ate in silence for a while.

The male peacock entertained us with a feather display and squawking. The female ignored the show and pecked the ground.

Gina eyed the peacocks before putting down her fork. "Phoenix, I've known since Christmas that you've been torn between these two guys. Let's take them one at a time. Start with Mike."

I took a deep breath and tried to gather my thoughts. "He's a lovely man who seemed considerate, at least until he threw that temper tantrum." I put down my fork. "I like his great sense of humor."

Kat smiled. "A guy who can make you laugh is an asset."

"He's also sexy and good looking." Latishia winked before wiping her mouth.

I nodded. "I have deep feelings for Mike. I'm not sure how deep. Going through a near-death experience sorta bonded us, but I'm not sure I'm 'in love' with him. Recent events have me wondering if I even know the true him."

Kat looked over the top of her glasses. "I guess it could've been life or death if the paramedics hadn't been there. From what I saw, only your lips swelled up a bit from an allergic reaction to shrimp. I'll admit, it was a heck of a first date."

Latishia chuckled. "You mean she had grouper lips. She looked like a plastic surgeon overloaded her with cosmetic fillers."

Gina rolled her eyes. "That's neither here nor there. I hear a 'but' coming."

I threw up my hands in frustration. "Mike's pushy. He's set on marriage, and I feel like a woman being herded by a sheepdog toward the altar. Which is annoying. I'm not sure I love him to the degree a wife should love a husband. It's a constant 'when we get married' this and 'when we get married' that. The latest complication has really thrown me for a loop."

Latishia asked around a mouth full of food, "There's more?"

I rubbed my eyes to keep myself from crying. "He recently told me Rachael caught Mark in a tawdry affair."

"Uh, oh," Gina said. "Sounds like his daughter needs a divorce attorney. Give her my number."

I nodded. "I already did, as well as a list of local psychologists. I'm hoping they'll work it out for the baby's sake. I have a sinking feeling if Rachael divorces Mark, she may move in with Mike. Don't get me wrong, I like his daughter, and I feel for her situation."

Gina nodded. "It would be difficult to be thrown into the role of an instant grandmother. I'm not sure I'd adjust to that easily."

I gulped some wine. "The family dynamics make it worse. To Mike, his daughter is the universe. His grandchild is the second most important thing in his life. So, I will always be third. Except on Saturday, when golf is third. Then I'd be relegated to fourth place."

No one said a word for several moments. My friends focused on their plates or on the peacock's showy seduction. I sliced some veggies, crammed them into my mouth, and chewed away my angst.

Latishia cleared her throat, breaking the silence. "Girl, I don't blame you for being upset. If I couldn't be number one, I'd at least want to come before golf."

"I didn't realize all this was happening with Mike. What about Brent?" Kat asked, cleaning her glasses on her blouse.

I swallowed. The chewed veggies felt like a bowling ball going down. "He's a fun guy who is loving and affectionate at times," I said.

Latishia gave me a bawdy wink. "He's also sexy and good looking."

I felt my face bloom with heat. "True."

"But..." all three said at once.

"At home, he's glued to his computer. I'm convinced he's married to the Internet, so I'd be the mistress."

Gina wagged her finger back and forth. "Not good. I often see divorces centered around the issues of Internet and gaming addictions."

"There's more," I said. "Hints have been dropped that if something happened to his dad, his mother couldn't live alone. Brent only has one married sister with two kids to share the load. She lives in New York."

Gina sipped some wine, placed it on the table, and leaned forward. "Why can't his mom live alone? Is she disabled or something?"

I shook my head. "She's an incredibly needy and dependent woman who's also a narcissist with a borderline personality disorder. She's not my first choice for a mother-in-law."

Latishia swallowed and pointed her fork at me. "She wouldn't be my choice of a mother-in-law, either. However, if Brent lives in Seattle, he won't be here to take care of her."

"True, but his mom doesn't get along with his sister. If forced to make a choice, the woman would choose her son. She dotes on him."

Kat's brow knitted as she leaned forward to pat my hand. "How ill is Brent's dad?"

"He's had one heart attack, and his COPD has slowed his recovery. He's going to a special clinic in Huntsville for treatments."

The corners of Kat's mouth turned down. "That's pretty serious. On the bright side, I've heard positive reports about that particular clinic."

My stomach lurched. I put down my eating utensils and pushed away my plate. "The question is, do I want to disrupt my whole life for Brent?" I put my face in my hands. When I glanced up, my friends looked at me with concerned expressions.

"How much change are you talking about?" Latishia asked, spearing a bite of potato.

"I'd have to sell my private practice, which may not be easy."

"What about all your patients?" Kat asked. "Would you transfer them to another psychologist?"

"That's another complication." I rubbed my temples. A headache started pounding inside my forehead. "In addition, I'd have to apply for a license in Washington State, which would take time. I could be there for months before being approved. Licensing boards typically meet only once a quarter."

Gina sat back in her chair. The sun backlit her dark curls, leaving an auburn halo around her. "It's always harder for a professional woman to move. You'd have to join a practice or start all over with your own. How long does it take to build up a sustainable patient load?"

"Depending on the area, it could be as long as a year. I'm a provider for several insurance companies, so that would help."

Latishia smacked her lips and set down her napkin. "I didn't know owning a business was so complicated. My parents make it look easy."

"There's more to owning a business than you can imagine. If Seattle is like Huntsville, I'd have to get a business license from both the city and county," I said.

Gina set down her wine and pointed her index finger at me. "Don't forget you'd have to find an office location and get the utilities turned on. I still think it might be easier to work for someone else or join an existing practice."

I could feel my frustration rising. *Or is it a hot flash?* "That's not all. On the personal side, I'd have to sell my home, which I love. Then,

I'd have to find a new medical doctor, dentist, and vet for Buffy. I'm not sure I want to uproot my entire life to live in the depression capital of the United States for *any* man." I undid a couple of buttons on my blouse. By now, I was on a full roast. I dabbed at my face with the napkin.

Gina frowned. "Not counting the fact that you'd be leaving us."

Gina's observation silenced the table.

CHAPTER 12: Machu Picchu

Early the next morning, André and a driver took us forty minutes up the road to Ollantaytambo Station to catch the train to Machu Picchu. Once on the train, I was happy to see the passengers would be sitting at booths for four that lined both sides of the cars.

The Divas chose a booth on the side that faced the Urubamba River.

"Since you like rivers, Phoenix, did you know this is the same river that runs behind our hotel?" Kat asked with a sly smile.

I looked out the train window. "Can't be. It has a different name."

Kat laughed, sliding into the window seat. "André told me the river has multiple names."

"Doesn't surprise me," Gina said. "Huntsville does the name game all the time. Some of our main roads have three or four different names. It drives newcomers to the area crazy."

Latishia squeezed into the seat next to Kat and fingered the bright turquoise table runner. "I hope we find these somewhere. I want one for my dining table."

I took the other window seat, so I could snap photos. "I'm sure we'll have plenty of shopping opportunities. I plan to buy an alpaca sweater when I get back to the hotel."

The train lunged to a start. The soothing rocking motion combined with the rhythmic sound of the wheels turning eased my tension.

We admired the changing view while drinks and a snack were served. The morning light highlighted thin fog banks along the shore. I was surprised to not see any wildlife along the shores of the muddy, tumbling river.

Two hours later, we arrived at Machu Picchu. When we exited the train, we searched for someone holding an Incan Elite sign.

A line formed between Gina's brows. "I don't see our guide." She craned her neck to look over and around the folks exiting the train.

I pointed. "Everyone seems to be going in one direction. Let's follow the crowd."

When we reached the bottom of the incline, we spotted the familiar sign.

I stepped forward and gestured to include the Divas. "Are you our guide?" I handed him my tour documents.

After glancing at them, he smiled. "Sí. Welcome to Machu Picchu. My name is Basilio."

After introductions, he said, "I suggest you use the restroom before you board the bus to the ruins."

We took his advice and dutifully deposited the toilet paper in the trash.

When we returned, he handed us bus tickets. "You must board the bus at the correct time. If you miss your bus, you can't board another because it will be full." He looked at his watch. "Yours is due to arrive in fifteen minutes." He pointed to an area where tourists congregated. "It will pick you up over there. They will take half of your ticket. Keep the other half so you can board any bus to come back here. You will have time to shop before the train leaves." He handed us train tickets. "These are for your trip home. You board at five. Don't wait until the last minute, and be careful to board the correct train. André will meet you at the Ollantaytambo Station and drive you back to the hotel." He waved and left.

Kat stowed her train tickets in her fanny pack and gestured toward the bus stop. "I don't know about y'all, but I plan to go wait for our ride up the mountain."

We followed in her wake. A line of buses waited to take tourists up to the ruin. When ours arrived, we surrendered half of our tickets. We clutched our return tickets and boarded the vehicle to search for window seats. When the bus was full, our driver closed the door and wound up the curvy road, narrowly missing his colleagues on the way down.

"This is beautiful," Gina said while leaning across me for a better view. "I have dibs on copies of all your photos of this trip."

I grinned. "I'll share all my photos with everyone."

"Good. I can't believe how green everything is," Latishia said.

"Me, either." I pointed at a peak, feeling the wonder of the scenery. "Look how steep it is. It must have taken centuries of erosion to achieve this."

Wisps of fog played along the narrow valleys, softening the sharp edges of rocks peeping from the lush vegetation. It was like a different world from the one I knew.

Thirty minutes later, the bus stopped. We stepped off and joined the swell of people jostling toward the ruin's entrance.

I scanned the crowd, hoping to spot our tour guide. The tour guides for larger groups held tall poles with waving flags or umbrellas hoisted into the air, while they led their flock toward the entrance. I nudged Gina and pointed. "There's an Incan Elite sign."

A short, trim guy in his early twenties greeted us. His backpack and hiking boots looked worn. After he verified our documents, he said, "I'm Roberto. Welcome to Machu Picchu. There are no restrooms at the ruins. I recommend you visit them here."

The Divas never miss a chance for a restroom break.

When we returned, Roberto led us to the entrance and produced our tickets for admittance. Once inside, he pulled us to the side. "This Incan citadel was built in the 15th century and later abandoned."

"Why?" Kat asked.

"We are not sure."

I shifted closer. "Was it because of the conquistadors?"

Roberto shook his head. "They never reached the city. The latest theory is it was abandoned after an outbreak of smallpox."

Kat shivered. "Nasty stuff. The white man's gift to many native populations." Our personal medical expert asked us, "Did y'all know the Europeans infected Native Americans with not only smallpox, but the bubonic plague and cholera?"

Latishia rolled her eyes. "Thank you, nurse Kat." She winked at Roberto. "If you're smart, you won't get her started. That little woman has encyclopedic medical knowledge."

Kat huffed and turned away.

Roberto gestured for us to follow him and took off at a brisk pace.

I rushed to keep up, panting like Buffy on a blistering day. "What is the Incan Trail?"

He stopped and smiled. "It is the trek from Cusco to here. It passes the Inca ruins of Llactapata, Runkurakay, Sayacmarca, and Phuyupatamarca."

I thought, *That's a mouthful.*

Gina trudged up the hill and caught up with us. "Cusco! That's a long way from here."

"Sí."

How long is the trail?" Kat asked.

"About forty-three kilometers."

"Which is?" Kat asked, pushing up her sleeves.

"Twenty-six miles." Roberto stood taller and raised his chin. "Most people hike it in four days. I did it in one."

We stopped and gawked at him.

Kat placed her hands on her hips and cocked her head. "You ran that far at this altitude in one day?"

His pleased smile widened. "Yes." The smile faltered. "Unfortunately, I didn't win the race."

Latishia leaned against a rock, her bosom heaving.

Our guide's gaze locked on her chest.

Fanning her face, Latishia said, "Lordy, I may not make it to the top."

The remainder of his smile vanished. "You must take your time. You are not used to this altitude. It is almost 8,000 feet above sea level." He moved closer and lowered his voice. "People have died up here. They try to cover it up, but it happens."

While we waited for Latishia to recover her breath, I again adjusted the digging straps of my backpack.

We started the climb up the first set of stairs. Each stone step was a struggle for me. The only one not suffering was Roberto, who leaped up them like a randy mountain goat in search of his true love.

"How tall were the Incans?" Gina gasped.

Roberto stopped to let us catch up. "It is believed the average man was five-foot two inches tall, and the average woman was four-foot nine."

Latishia fanned herself despite the chilly day. "Sweet baby Jesus, I'm about to spout lava at any minute."

Roberto's brows hiked up his face. He appraised her before looking at me, concern etching his youthful visage.

"She'll be okay in a moment. It's a woman thing." I whispered.

He nodded, watching Latishia with wide eyes.

Kat touched his arm. "I don't get it. All these steps are about one to two feet tall. Why did they make them this size if they were so short?"

"I was wondering the same thing," Latishia said. She stopped fanning and wiped the sweat from her face with a tissue.

Roberto shrugged. "I do not know."

When we reached the top of the first viewing area, the terraces spread out below us. The landscape was a masterpiece of vibrant green, grey stone, brilliant blue skies, and drifting wispy clouds.

Roberto held out his hand. "If you will give me your cameras and phones, I will take your photos."

When we finished the photo session, Latishia said, "At least I have proof I made it this far. That should impress Dante."

Kat chuckled. "Can anything a parent does impress a preteen boy?"

Latishia gave the landscape a once over. "How many steps are there?"

Roberto's face broke into a sheepish grin. "Only sixteen hundred."
We groaned in unison.

Latishia moaned while struggling up a big step. "I need to lose some weight and get in shape."

"I've been telling you that for over a year now," Kat said with a smug grin.

Latishia glared at her. Pointing a manicured nail, she said, "Keep it up, little woman, and I'll sit on you."

Kat waved her off. "You'd have to catch me first."

We struggled up more stairs made from giant stone blocks. I had to focus all my attention on where I stepped to avoid slipping on them. So many people had climbed those giant steps over the centuries that they had become both slick and uneven.

I sagged a bit when we stopped at a wall with a doorway. The large stones of different sizes were fitted together precisely. It was hard to imagine how they managed it during those ancient times. A mammoth rectangular lintel loomed above the doorway.

Kat ran her hand across one of the stones. "How did they get that huge one up there?"

Roberto looked up at the lintel. "There have been many theories, but no conclusions."

Latishia shaded her eyes with her hand when the sun poked through a cloud bank. "Looks like it would weigh as much as a small car."

Roberto pulled a diagram of the doorway out of his backpack. He showed us an artist rendering of how a wooden gate could be attached.

We worked our way down more rock stairs, terraces, and rooms to an open area. Drifting wisps of clouds skidded across the indigo sky. Machu Picchu seemed to go on and on. *I wonder what this looked like with crops on the terraces and roofs on the buildings?*

I'd begun to wonder if I could possibly climb up or down one more step, when the tour ended.

When we exited the park, Roberto showed us a cafeteria and handed us a pass for lunch. Before saying goodbye, he pointed to where tourists boarded buses to go back down the mountain. "Don't lose the second half to your tickets."

Latishia watched him leave while shifting from one foot to the other. I suspected I knew why.

"I don't know about y'all, but my bladder is about to embarrass me."

"I'm with you," Gina said, before taking off for the restroom.

Kat and I followed. Relieved, yet still hungry, we headed toward the restaurant.

Latishia rubbed her hands together. "Now this is a buffet. After all that exercise, I need a fill-up."

With full plates, we weaved between tables until we found an empty one. I eased into my seat. From the moans and groans of my companions, their muscles and joints must be complaining as much as mine.

"We sound like a bunch of old biddies," I said.

Gina picked up her fork. She pointed it at me with a gleam of malice in her eyes. "I feel like an old biddy that's been run over by a paving machine. Don't mess with me."

"I don't know about y'all, but I plan to make use of the whirlpool in my room tonight," Kat said while rubbing the top of one leg.

The idea brought a smile to all our faces.

A Peruvian group of three musicians began playing the guitar, lute, and skin drum. They wore bright wool ponchos with Incan designs and wool caps of bright colors with pom poms hanging down each side of their faces.

Latishia nudged Kat and pointed toward the musicians. "Do you think Dante would wear one of those hats?"

Kat chuckled. "Jack wouldn't be caught dead in it."

Latishia considered the idea a moment. "What about Aaron?"

I laughed. "Can you even imagine Aaron in one of those? I doubt you could find one big enough to fit his head."

Latishia's lower lip poked out. "Are you saying my Aaron is big-headed?"

I choked on a bite of lamb. Snatching my bottle of water, I tried to wash down the lump of meat. *That didn't come out right.* I shook my head. "I'm saying he has big everything. The man is an ebony Hercules."

Gina giggled with a mouthful of food. She covered her mouth with a napkin and swallowed. "You've never told us. How big is it?" She raised both brows and gave Latishia an expectant look.

Latishia crossed her arms. "Girl, you act like I should take a tape measure to bed. We've discussed this before, so don't go there again."

"Just curious. I can't imagine a man that size would have a tiny weenie," Gina said with a sly smile.

I knew that smile. *Gina's having fun baiting her.*

"Don't you be worrying your pea brain about his weenie. In fact, I'm beginning to wonder about your fascination." Latishia picked up her fork and gave her full attention to her mound of different desserts.

After lunch, we rode the bus down to the modern city of Machu Picchu. The roaring Urubamba River ran through the middle of town between the two stone walls that reinforced the banks. Bridges allowed access to both sides. Both shores were decorated with monuments and statues.

"It's pretty," I said. "But it's a tourist trap. Look at all those stores."

Latishia grabbed me by the arm and dragged me behind her toward the shops. Gina and Kat followed.

Kat said, "Shop fast. We don't have much time."

An hour later, we trudged toward the train station. I felt spent, both physically and financially.

We eased into seats at the station to wait. The only part of my body that didn't hurt was my eyebrows. "I'm ready to settle down on the train, eat a snack, and nap."

Our train arrived on schedule. Pain sliced through my muscles and tendons when I climbed the stairs to the train. From the relieved looks on my friends' faces, they were as glad as I was to slide into the seats around our table.

Kat insisted we sanitize the area.

I settled in and enjoyed the scenery while shooting some photos. The afternoon glow created a different world from the misty morning vistas. There was something about the lighting in these mountains that was magical.

Sometime later, the staff delivered a drink and snack. It was just the pick-me-up I needed, since it looked like we would miss dinner.

I was napping when the pounding of drums jarred me awake. My eyes snapped open. Struggling to an upright position, I glanced around and tried to locate the noise.

Gina blinked while wiping drool off her chin.

Kat sat up and rubbed her eyes. Looking concerned, she shoved her glasses into place. "Sounds like the natives are restless."

"Sweet Baby Jesus!" Latishia covered her proud bosom with both hands. "Are we under attack?"

A man wearing a brightly colored jaguar mask, complete with fangs, jumped into our train car, causing a few startled women to scream. His costume included a multicolored shirt with beads, a long white disheveled wig, gloves that looked like claws, and a sizeable, rattling striped staff of multiple hues. He shook it vigorously while dancing down the aisle. Occasionally, he lunged, causing the startled passengers to squeal.

Kat whipped out her phone and started videoing the performance. Not to be outdone, we followed her example.

When it was over, we settled back into our seats and put away our phones. The sun dropped out of sight and plunged us into darkness.

Latishia grinned. "I can't wait to show that video to Dante."

Kat was still smiling. "I think Jack will like it, too."

It was eight o'clock when we arrived back at Ollantaytambo Station. I peered out the window. "It's raining."

"Great," Gina replied with her most sarcastic tone. Her long curls tend to double in volume in wet weather. She dug through her purse and pulled out a scrunchy.

Within minutes, she'd constrained her hair, wrapped it into a bun, and pinned it with the scrunchy. I have never understood how she achieves those results. I've tried many times and failed with each attempt.

When we stepped off the train, André stepped forward to claim us. He led the way through the crowd to a parking area where our driver sat in the rain-speckled van. We were all damp by the time we settled into our seats and fastened the safety belts. Kat pulled out a couple of wipes, and we cleaned.

The crowded gravel parking area teemed with cars and motorcycles trying to claim passengers from the train. It took twenty minutes to drive half a block to exit the parking lot.

Drooping from exhaustion, I only wanted to slouch in my seat and maybe nap. That wasn't to be, because our new driver preferred to drive down the centerline of the two-lane road, only shifting into his lane at the last minute for oncoming traffic.

Gina reached over and grabbed my hand while she whispered prayers.

Latishia leaned forward and said, "The centerline is there for a reason, and it's not for you to drive down. Shouldn't you get in your lane?"

The driver only responded with, "Too bumpy."

The headlights of a large approaching vehicle blinded me.

Latishia shouted, "Get in your lane!"

I scrambled to tighten my seatbelt. My heart pounded against my chest wall, seeking to escape. *Move over. Move over. Move over*, I chanted in my mind.

Our driver continued down the centerline.

Gina looked at me, her eyes round with alarm. "What the hell is he doing? Playing chicken?"

The lights grew larger and brighter.

I tried to control the tremble in my voice as I strove for a commanding tone. "If you don't get this van in the correct lane and keep it there, I'll report you to Incan Elite Tours and Peru Tourism!"

André spoke a few words of Spanish.

The driver shifted back into his lane. It was a little too close for my comfort. The massive tour bus rocked the van when it passed.

"Merda!" Gina slumped into her seat.

Kat, her face pale in the blue light from the dash, mouthed, Thank you.

Latishia sat with crossed arms, glaring at the back of the driver's head. I felt sure acid-laced words were running through her mind, ones her Baptist minister wouldn't like.

The driver's expression, reflected in the rearview mirror, showed no concern.

We pulled into the drive at our hotel at nine o'clock. My muscles were so tight, I wasn't sure I could get out of my seat.

I half-limped and half-waddled my way toward the hotel's door. My legs felt like metal utility poles. Bending them to walk up the few steps to enter the lobby was excruciating. My only thoughts centered around the bottle of Aleve and the hydro tub in my room. From the groans of my friends, I knew I wasn't the only one suffering from climbing steep stone steps.

We hobbled into the lobby and over to the desk. The clerk on duty offered us bottles of chilled water.

Latishia uncapped hers. "I may never move again if I sit down."

Someone jumped up from a sofa in the dim lobby and hurried our way.

"Phoenix!"

We all turned.

Brent stepped out of the shadows.

CHAPTER 13: The Big Surprise

The unopened water bottle slipped from my grip and bounced on the tile floor.

Brent rushed forward and wrapped me in his arms.

I sucked in a breath. *Brent? Here?*

Behind me, Gina said, "Merda," under her breath.

Squashed to the point of near suffocation, I managed to squeak, "Can't breathe."

When he released me, the open-mouthed expression on Latishia's face was the first thing I saw over his shoulder.

"What are you doing here?" popped out of my mouth. I steadied my breathing while shoving damp hair into place.

Brent gave my upper arms a little shake and smiled down at me. "Are you surprised?"

"Well, yes." *And confused. I would've been home in a few days.* "It's a long and expensive trip. Why are you here? Are you starting a vacation before you move?"

Brent just stood there, grinning down at me.

Gina strolled over to stand beside me and crossed her arms. "Answer Phoenix. Why are you here, Brent?" Using her best attorney tone, she sounded like she was questioning a wayward husband on a witness stand.

Ignoring her, Brent said, "You're right. It is a long way. It seems like I've been on a plane for ages. When I started this adventure, I never realized it would take five flights and a car ride to get to this hotel."

Kat came closer. "How did you know we were at this hotel today?"

"If Phoenix hadn't left me her itinerary, I wouldn't have known where to find y'all."

My mouth was so dry, my tongue felt superglued to the roof of my mouth. My vision blurred. I shook my head to clear it. "Believe me, I understand how you feel. I was sick of plane flights, too. You still haven't told me why you're here."

He ran both hands through his tousled hair. "I came to apologize for my texts. Mom said I should've waited until you arrived home. I was so hyped about the promotion and moving to Seattle that I couldn't wait to tell you." He smacked himself on the side of his head. "She told me you probably thought I wanted you to live with me without the benefit of marriage."

That did enter my mind.

He grasped both of my hands before dropping to one knee.

I felt dizzy and sick to my stomach. My heart lodged in my throat, making it difficult to breathe. I swallowed hard.

"Phoenix, will you marry me?"

CHAPTER 14: What Happened?

Everything was a blur. I blinked a few times before the vaulted wood ceiling came into focus. Latishia kept repeating, "Lord, please don't let her die of altitude sickness."

Goodness, am I dying? Where am I?

An angry-looking Gina suddenly loomed over me. She fanned me with a magazine, while Kat took my pulse.

I'm on a sofa in the lobby. But what happened? Something clicked into place, and I remembered.

Gina disappeared from view and Brent leaned over me, his brows drawn together. "Is she all right? What happened?"

Kat felt my forehead. "I think it's a combination of shock and overexertion at high altitudes. She may also be dehydrated and have low blood sugar. We went up to Machu Picchu today, and our day started early. We only had a small snack on the way back." She stood and looked him in the eye. "Do you have a room here?"

He flushed a bit. "Um, well, no. I thought I'd stay with Phoenix." He winked at me and grinned.

I didn't smile back. *He planned to do some celebrating in my bed tonight. Not! I can barely walk.*

Kat said, "I think Phoenix is pretty done in for now. I suggest you get a room for tonight and discuss your proposal tomorrow morning." She took him by the arm and pulled him toward the registration desk.

Grateful to Kat, I sat up and held a hand to my head to stop the wooziness. My stomach tumbled like an Olympic gymnast. *Phoenix O'Leary, don't you dare get sick in this lobby. Deep breathe.*

"Wouldn't it be better if I stayed with her tonight to make sure she's okay?" Brent asked, looking back at me over his shoulder.

"All she needs is quiet and rest, with no distractions. I'm sure you want what's best for Phoenix right now." Kat turned and told Gina, "Y'all take her back to her room and get some water down her. I'll be there in a minute to check on her."

Gina and Latishia helped me stand. I wavered and reached for Gina's shoulder to steady myself, while I swallowed down the bile inching up my throat. When I felt capable of moving, I said, "Ready."

Gina and Latishia held my arms like I might sink to the floor at any minute.

"I think I'm okay now. I feel sick to my stomach, but I don't know why."

We had moved maybe a hundred feet when a boisterous wave of heat traveled from my gut to my face. I felt like a roaring fire in a hearth full of logs. "Hot flash," I mumbled. Sweat dotted my brow and upper lip.

Gina tugged on my arm and said, "Let's get her outside where it's cooler."

Once there, the cool, fragrant breeze caressed my damp face while I struggled to shed my jacket.

Latishia helped me take it off. "Sweet Baby Jesus, I thought you'd had a heart attack or something. One minute you were standing; the next, you crumpled into a heap at Brent's feet. It took a good ten years off my life."

I glanced over at Gina, who didn't look worried. She looked pissed. "Quell' uomo stupido."

"What?" Latishia looked exasperated.

Gina rolled her eyes. "I said, that stupid man. He flies to Peru and shows up unannounced when we'll be leaving in a couple of days to go home. Then, he proposes in the lobby of a hotel. Puleeese."

I chuckled. "It wasn't the most romantic proposal I've ever had, but coming all this way is kinda amorous."

Gina frowned as she took my arm. "Okay, I'll give him points for coming to Peru."

We struggled like the rusty-jointed Tin Man in the Wizard of Oz along the winding garden paths. Our stiff muscles made the journey anything but graceful. The landscaping was artistically lit to highlight trees, statues, and flowers in large clay pots lying on their sides. If I hadn't been so exhausted, I could've enjoyed it more.

The journey up two flights of stairs was excruciating. Each step up was accompanied by our moans and groans. When we arrived at my room, I felt a bit unsteady again. They gripped my arms tighter and walked me to my bed. I sat down and looked up at them. "What am I going to do about Brent?"

"Nothing," Kat said as she hobbled into the room. "At least not tonight. Here, I found you a banana."

She thrust it in my face like a loaded penis before looking at Gina. "Would you fill up her whirlpool bath, please?"

Gina nodded before disappearing into the bathroom.

I took the banana in a trembling hand.

"Latishia, please get her a bottle of water. She needs to hydrate."

Latishia disappeared to begin her search.

Kat turned back to me and took my pulse. Smiling, she said. "Much better. The incident downstairs threw you for a loop. Threw me for one, too. I've never seen you faint."

I placed my hand on my forehead and sank back onto the bed. "What am I going to do?"

"You could start by eating the banana. The sugar and potassium will help you." Kat climbed on the bed beside me and sat cross-legged. "I know we discussed this at lunch a day or so ago. You voiced several issues but never said for sure what you planned to do about Brent's offer to move to Seattle."

Gina rushed in from the bathroom. "Wait, I want to hear this."

"Me, too," Latishia said from the doorway, a bottle of water in her hand. She came over and gave it to me.

I shifted to mimic Kat's cross-legged position. "I'd planned to say he deserved a woman who was willing to give up everything to follow him to Seattle, but I wasn't the one." I rubbed my face. "Now, I'm not sure. He came all this way to propose. That should count for something, shouldn't it? I'm confused about what to do."

I peeled the banana, took a bite, and chewed.

Gina perched on the side of the bed. "How much he loves you is only half the equation. I've handled too many divorces where my clients told me they weren't a hundred percent sure they were making the correct decision before they married. Some even said they had doubts while standing in front of the minister."

I nodded. "Makes sense. I've heard the same from my patients."

"That's why I'm not letting Aaron rush me," Latishia said. "I want some of the new to rub off the relationship and see how we both feel."

"At the very least, tell Brent you'll consider it before saying yes." Gina said. She nudged me. "Remember Todd and all the trauma he put you through during the divorce."

I choked down the fruit and coughed. I washed the rest down with some water.

"Jeez, did you have to bring him up and ruin my night?"

Gina arched a brow. "Just saying…."

Latishia nodded. "Mama always told me, 'act in haste, and you'll repent in leisure.' Don't let Brent rush you. See what he says tomorrow."

"Then it's settled. You can work it out tomorrow at eight when you meet Brent for breakfast." Kat smiled and gave my knee a little pat of reassurance. "Finish the banana, drink all the water, take an Aleve, and get in the whirlpool tub for a soak."

I saluted. "Yes, Sergeant."

Kat climbed off the bed and winked. "Don't you mean General?" she asked before shooing Gina and Latishia toward the door.

Latishia's lower lip protruded. "Give that little woman a medical emergency, and she gets downright bossy."

Gina chuckled and put an arm around Latishia's shoulders. "Ain't that the truth?"

They called goodbyes before the door closed.

CHAPTER 15: *The Big Talk*

The next morning, I woke renewed and refreshed, though I wasn't looking forward to breakfast with Brent. Still stiff, I moved like the Tin Man before someone oiled his joints. My joints weren't the problem. It was my muscles and tendons. I felt like someone had restrung me with rubber bands that were too short. To my relief, the more I moved, the better I felt.

Brent stood waiting by the door when I entered the dining room. His tight mouth and jumping jaw muscle relayed his tension.

He took my hand and squeezed it. "Are you feeling better?"

"Oh, yes." I gestured toward the extensive breakfast buffet. "I'm famished. Dinner was only a banana and a bottle of water."

He leaned down and kissed me. "You scared me last night." His hand ran up and down my back, causing an involuntary shiver.

I chuckled. "I scared myself. When I opened my eyes, I wasn't sure where I was at first."

"I never once imagined that when I proposed, my future bride would faint. I was looking up into your beautiful green eyes, and a second later you were on the floor."

I examined my shoes, unsure what to say. "I'm truly sorry. Let's eat first and then talk, unless you want me to swoon again."

"No way. Kat might show up." He rubbed his upper arm. "That little woman has a body builder's grip. I didn't want to abandon you last night, but once she latched on, she was determined to take me to the check-in desk."

I chuckled. General Kat.

His phone binged. After wrestling it from his jeans pocket, he looked at the screen and frowned.

"Bad news?"

"It's Mom. She wanted to wish me a good morning. She probably wants an update. I didn't tell her I saw you last night."

The restaurant was busy. We ambled toward a stack of plates, passing snatches of conversation in English and Spanish.

He handed me a pristine white plate. "I'm starving. You better go first."

Chuckling, I accepted it. "Afraid you won't leave any food for me?"

The first section contained different cold meats and cheeses. I loaded my plate with plenty of protein. The second section held different types of breads. I chose a flaky croissant. The third held fruits, some of which were unfamiliar. Not wanting to miss anything, I picked a sample of each.

I spotted Brent settling into a chair at a secluded table in the corner. *How did he get all that food and finish before me?*

He frowned at his phone again.

I walked over and set down my plate. "Your Mom?"

He nodded and shoved his phone into his shirt pocket.

I eyed his plate piled high with some of everything. "I can see you're hungry. I need coffee."

"Me, too. I was too tired to sleep and worried about you to boot."

The coffee area contained urns of caffeinated and decaf coffee, hot water for tea, and an urn of hot milk. I chose a café con leche and was pleased to see packets of stevia.

I joined Brent back at the table. I eased down with a groan, before stirring stevia into my brew.

He took a gulp of his black brew and screwed up his face. "Wow, that's strong enough to sprout hair on every inch of my body."

I couldn't help but laugh at the vision of a Bigfoot version of Brent.

We both dug in, oohing and ahhing over the tasty items on our plates. Brent seemed satisfied to leave the serious discussion of matrimony under the table at present.

The Divas entered the dining area and headed for the buffet. Latishia already had a big smile plastered on her face. Kat headed straight to the refreshment area for a cup of tea. Only Gina looked around until she spotted me. Once we'd locked gazes, she nodded and picked up a plate. After they served themselves, they sat across the expansive room from us. I knew if things went awry, the Divas had my back, or in this case, my front.

Brent's phone pinged. He gave an exasperated sigh and pulled it out of his pocket to check it. He shook his head and put it face down on the table.

He cleared his throat and sat back in his chair. "Phoenix, I'm not sure what happened last night, but I got the feeling you weren't a hundred percent happy to see me."

Oh, boy. Here we go. I shifted in my seat to face him, while I decided how to approach the subject. "There were a lot of factors you need to consider. I'd had a long, arduous day, at high altitude, and I was dehydrated, which made it all worse."

"I understand all that, but my reception wasn't quite what I expected."

I ran my finger around the brim of my coffee cup. "What were you expecting?"

He flung his hands in the air. "I don't know, maybe that you'd rush into my arms, kiss me, and tell me how happy you were that I flew for hours to come see you. After all, I asked you to join me in Seattle. Instead, you stared at me like I was a ghost or something, and then asked me why I was here."

My ire rose. "In my defense, you appeared out of the dark. I was shocked to see you. A bit of warning would've helped."

He nodded and looked through the wall of glass at the pool. His jaw muscle was jumping again.

I fortified myself with some coffee and looked across the room toward the Divas. They were looking at us over the brims of their mugs. *I need to steer this conversation to a less emotional place.*

"Tell me about your promotion."

Brent perked up and described his new management position with responsibility over five programmers' work.

"The best part is I'll still be doing some programming. If I do well, I'll have a chance to move up to my boss's position when he retires in two years. He supervises over twenty programmers."

I nodded, happy for his success. "I'm assuming this will mean a raise?"

"More than I expected. Some of the extra salary was added because the cost of living in Seattle is higher."

"Makes sense. Have you found a place to live yet?"

He shook his head. "I plan to go out next week and scout out some options. I'd like to live closer to work to avoid long commutes. I kinda wanted to put that decision off until we could choose a place together." He smiled and wiggled his brows.

I rubbed circles on my churning stomach.

"What do your parents think about your move across the country?"

The phone pinged. His jaw muscle flexed again. He glared at it as if he wanted to throw it across the room.

I knew I'd hit on a sensitive subject. I imagined his mother throwing herself at his feet in a hysterical fit while moaning, "My baby!"

"Mom was real upset at first. Dad said she cried for days. The poor guy finally relented and agreed to sell their house, so they can move to Seattle."

One of the warning flags in my brain did a frantic wave. A tiny voice yelled, *run!*

"You told me their house is paid off. How're they going to afford to live out there on their retirement income?" I asked.

"They're in Seattle now, looking at independent living facilities. If they can't afford anything, we may join finances and buy a house together. They can live in a section of it." He scowled at his phone as if daring it to ping again. It did.

He snatched it up.

I could see the screen. There was a string of texts from his mother.

No way. I'm not living with an emotionally dependent, narcissistic woman with a borderline personality disorder. No! No! No!

"Sorry about the interruptions. Mom's a bit unsettled right now. I asked her to stop texting until I call her."

"I see. Please understand that I'm flattered about your proposal. I apologize again for fainting."

His brow creased. "Passing out wasn't the reaction I expected."

I chuckled. "It was a surprise for me, too. I can't remember ever fainting before."

He reached across the table and took my hand. "I know I don't have a ring yet, but we can go pick one out when we get home. Heck, we can even look here if you want." His thumb ran over my knuckles. He leaned close, his coffee-scented breath tickling my ear, and whispered, "You never told me your answer."

My heart pounded in my ears. *Calm down,* I warned myself. *Remember his mother.*

I shifted to create some distance between us. "Before I do, I need for you to understand what this will mean for me emotionally, financially, and career-wise." I went through the same list I'd discussed with the Divas over lunch the day Brent had texted me with his good news.

He ran his hand over the stubble on his chin. "Phoenix, I had no idea how much of an impact a move to Seattle would have on your life. I guess I thought since your parents are deceased, that you'd have no ties to Huntsville. I'd forgotten about your practice and licensure."

I patted his hand. "The Divas and their parents have been my adopted family for years. I'm glad you understand." I stopped to gather my resolve. "Brent, you're a wonderful guy in many ways. You deserve a woman who'd be willing to throw it all away for you because her love for you is so deep."

He frowned and sat back. "Are you saying you don't love me?"

"I do care for you, but not enough to take on your mother and move to Seattle." I inhaled sharply. *There goes my mouth again.*

He slumped in his chair and pulled back his hand.

Oh, boy. Did I go too far? It's so hard to tell the truth and not be hurtful.

Brent sat quiet and stared out the window.

I waited, my heart doing a frantic tap dance in my chest. I swallowed some coffee and glanced across the room toward the Divas. Their gazes were glued on us.

He looked into my eyes. "To be honest, I didn't realize how much I cared for you until you left on this trip. I missed you every day. When the promotion and transfer came through, I felt sick knowing you might not be in my life anymore. As for my mother, I know she's a handful. I guess I'd hoped a psychologist would know how to deal with her."

Knowing how to deal with your mom and wanting to are two different things. I nodded. "I understand that you love me or you wouldn't be here. The truth is, while I love many things about you, I'm not *in love* with you. It took me this long to get past my emotional pain from Todd betraying me and divorcing me, so I could understand my feelings for you. I don't love you the way I should to marry you."

Tears welled in his eyes. He swiped at them with the back of his hand. "I appreciate your honesty. Marriage is serious business."

"True," I said. I sat back and cocked my head to the side. "Can we part friends?"

He nodded. "I'd like that."

Feeling relieved, I decided to change the subject. "Since you're in Peru, what are your plans?"

He shifted in his seat. "I think I'll contact a tour group and see Machu Picchu, as well as some of the other Incan sites. I have a week."

I suggested he go online and contact Peru Tourism. We sat for a few more minutes discussing things I'd seen that he might be interested in touring.

Brent's warm hand covered mine. "Before I go, I need to know if the reason you won't marry me is because you're in love with the other guy?"

I looked down to gather my thoughts and then met his gaze. "I'm just as conflicted about my feelings toward Mike. Part of the reason I took this trip was to gain some distance from both of you to help clarify my feelings."

He grinned. "That helps."

I rolled my eyes. "Men are so competitive."

He chuckled. "I'm blaming the testosterone."

He stood and pulled me into a hug. He squeezed tight as if he was trying to absorb my essence before he let go.

CHAPTER 16: What Now

After Brent left, I shambled on stiff limbs to the Divas' table with a fresh cup of café con leche.

Latishia did her neck thing. "Well? Are you going to tell us what happened or make us suffer?"

Gina made a slashing motion with her hand. "I have no intention of suffering. As Nonna would say, 'spill the beans.'"

I gave a Cliff Notes version of our discussion. When I got to the part where Brent wanted us to share a house with his parents, Gina shot out of her chair and flung her napkin on the table. It slid to the floor at her feet.

"È pazzo?" She snatched it up before plopping back into her seat. "He expected you to live in the same house with his parents! Pensavo fosse più intelligente di così."

Latishia rolled her eyes. "There she goes again, talking in Italian. Translation, please."

"I said, is he crazy? I thought he was smarter than that." Her hands waved around, expressing her frustration. "What woman with any sense starts a marriage by moving in with the mother-in-law from

Hell?" She leaned a forearm on the table. "What was going on with his phone? He kept checking it."

"His mother kept texting him," I said.

Gina snatched up her fork and stuck it into a cube of cheese. "Mama's boy."

"Calm down. Why are you so upset? I'm not marrying him," I said.

Gina has always been a bit of a mother hen toward me. She's several months older, and I think she sees it as her responsibility.

Kat took a sip of tea and eyed Gina. "Despite Mrs. Powers, I believe Brent is a lovely person, no matter what Gina says."

I nodded and was surprised when tears formed in my eyes. Reality hit me like a baseball bat jabbed into the gut. *I may never see Brent again.* I remembered the first time we made love. All the long talks we'd had since we met. The fun experiences we shared. It was all excellent—except for his mother. *Am I too picky?*

I wiped my eyes with the tissue Kat handed me. "I'm a Southern belle at heart. I wouldn't be happy living in Seattle. Too much rain to suit me."

Kat patted my back. "I suspect his mother would've driven you to murder."

"Or suicide." Gina swallowed the last of her coffee. "What does Brent plan to do now?"

I sniveled and blew my nose. "He plans to spend a week in Peru before heading to Seattle to find a place to live. I wished him all the best."

Kat stood and put her purse on her shoulder. "We need to finish our packing so André can take us to Cusco."

Back in my room, I loaded my suitcase and backpack. I knew in my heart I'd made the right decision. Brent's a fine man, but not the right one for me. Is Mike the right one? If not, will I ever find the right one?

I rolled my case to the stairs and hefted it down, one step at a time. I was a bit winded when I made it to the lobby. I stood in front of the beautiful stained-glass window, and for the last time, appreciated the symbolism in the design. This was the first time I'd visited a country that was financially poor and culturally rich at the same time.

The Divas arrived, looking a bit sad.

Latishia looked around the lobby. "I'm going to miss this place."

We did a group hug.

André walked in. "Are you ready to go to Cusco?"

We nodded and rolled our cases to the van. Urubamba looked less festive now that Carnival had ended. All the banners and decorations were gone, making the poverty and disrepair more apparent. We passed a thin woman wearing a robin's-egg blue jumper and a tall white hat with a wide black band.

Latishia said, "That's the first white hat I've seen."

We left the dusty town and drove through Sacred Valley, between two sets of mountains that took on a purple hue in the distance. Sometime later, while driving down a beige dirt road, we saw a man and a woman walking up the hill toward our van.

I shifted to take a photo through the windscreen. The woman wore a beige straw hat with a tall crown and a wide black band. Each of them had gathered a load of corn stalks in multi-colored striped blankets that rested against their backs. They held the blankets closed at their throats and were transporting the burden up the hill.

Kat also leaned forward. "Is that the normal way to bring in a crop?"

André turned to face us and rested his arm on the back of the seat. "It is if you're poor and you don't own a truck."

I sat back and thought about what I'd seen.

Two hours after we left the hotel, we arrived in Cusco.

André looked back over his shoulder. "We will tour Koricancha Temple and Plaza de Armas while Pedro takes your luggage to the Hotel Xima, which is where you'll stay tonight."

We exited the van and followed André to a narrow street of stones.

He stopped and pointed at a tall wall that ran down one side. "This is an Incan wall. They used ashlar masonry, which means it took longer to construct."

Latishia cocked her head to the side and squinted at one of the precise joints. "What is ashlar masonry?"

André ran his hand around one of the stones. "It's a construction method that uses similarly sized cubed stones. See how this stone is cut to fit perfectly with every stone around it"

The enormous square stones were interlocked together without the benefit of any fillers. I had no idea how many people or how long it took to construct it, but the wall was still solid despite the passage of time and multiple earthquakes. The sheer size and length of it made Kat look tiny when she stood next to it.

"Now we go to the Koricancha Temple," André said, after checking his watch.

We walked through the streets of the city, admiring the storefronts. Conversations in Spanish filled my ears as the acrid scent of car exhaust burned my nose.

André stopped and pointed at a church. "That is the Koricancha Temple."

Gina shaded her eyes. "Doesn't look like a temple. Looks more like a Catholic Church."

André nodded. "It was an Incan palace and sacred place. The Incas worshipped Inti, the Sun god, and had an altar inside where the stone curves."

Grinning, I poked Gina with my elbow. "Remember, the Catholic Church stomped out paganism in two ways. First, it stole their holidays by attaching Christian ones to the same days, and second, it built cathedrals on top of their destroyed temples."

I'm a recovering Catholic. Gina and I both grew up in the Holy Mother Church and attended parochial schools, so I could get away with teasing her.

André continued his spiel while we walked toward the building. "You're correct, Phoenix. The Spanish conquistadors destroyed most of the temple during the war that occurred in the 16th century. When the Dominicans arrived, they built a church on top of the foundation. It is now the Convent of Santo Domingo. You can see where the ashlar masonry is on the bottom."

When we arrived, I was surprised to see that the ashlar masonry wall wasn't just curved, the stones themselves were curved. *Amazing.*

Inside, large paintings represented the colonial period. André led us into an Incan ashlar masonry room with windows. "I want you to imagine every surface of this room covered with gold." He pulled out an artist's rendition of what he described. "Written records by the Spanish indicate this room once looked like this rendition."

"Wow." Latishia's eyes widened. "That's a lot of gold."

Gina shrugged, unimpressed. "That's only one room. The entire interior of St. Mark's Basilica in Venice is covered in gold mosaic tiles."

"Where did all the gold go?" Latishia asked, still staring at the page in his hands.

He closed the book. "The Spanish stole it."

André eventually carried us down to the area where the curved stone wall stood. He led us to a model that replicated the temple's interior. Pointing at the curved section, he said, "This is where they worshipped."

Kat looked from the model to the large curved stones. She strolled over, stood in the curve, and held out her arms. "Right here?"

André grinned. "If you were a sheep, you would be a blood sacrifice right now."

Kat hurried back to join us, her nose scrunched with distaste.

Latishia grinned. "As tiny as she is, it wouldn't be much of an offering."

Kat crossed her arms and eyed Latishia from top to bottom. "Are you saying you'd make a better sacrifice to the sun god?"

Gina chuckled. "Now, ladies. You'd both make worthy sacrifices."

André tried to hide his smile before waving for us to follow. "Let's go to the Plaza de Armas. It has a beautiful fountain. There you can see the Cathedral Basilica of the Assumption of the Virgin. It's the most important church in the city."

Latishia looked past me to Gina. "Why do some Catholic Churches have such long, complicated names?"

Gina shrugged. "I have no idea. Do I look like I'm the Pope?" She tapped André's shoulder. "Why is this basilica so important?"

"It is the mother church of the Roman Catholic Archdiocese of Cusco."

"That may answer your question, Latishia. The bigger, more important the church, the longer the name," I said.

When we arrived in the plaza, André swept his arm toward the cathedral. "As you can see, the building contains elements of Gothic, Baroque, and Renaissance architectural styles."

Kat gazed up and asked, "Would you call that eclectic architecture?"

Gina craned her neck to take in the impressive twin bell towers. "Kat, these churches took a long time to build. It wasn't unusual for an architect to die before the project was finished."

"That's true," I said. "Keep in mind, some churches didn't begin grand, but were added onto as centuries passed."

Gina was in her element. She loves touring churches, especially the large elaborate ones.

When we entered the cathedral, only occasional whispers interrupted the silence. The scent of incense filled the air, making my eyes water and itch. I rubbed them and sneezed. Everyone around me turned to glare. Several backed away.

Good grief, it was only a sneeze.

The nave had a high arched center section with multiple side chapels. Gina started on one side, examining each one. I was drawn down the center aisle to the sanctuary. The area behind the altar was an elaborate panel covered in gold and resplendent with carvings, paintings, and statuary.

André joined me and looked up.

"I could look at this for an hour and still not see all the complexities," I said.

Kat strolled over. "Is the altar silver?" she asked.

"Sí."

Latishia cocked her head to the side. "If I'd designed this, the altar would've been gold, too. I think the silver makes it look like an afterthought."

"The silver was donated. I think the church used what it had," André said, a bit haughty.

His tight mouth and unhappy expression made me think he didn't like Latishia's criticism. While the silver altar was beautiful, I agreed with Latishia. The golden back wall and the silver didn't blend well together.

Gina joined us. "This is a beautiful church."

André was all smiles again. "Come, you must see our famous painting of the Last Supper."

His mischievous grin had me wondering what he planned.

He pointed up toward a large oil painting. "It was painted in 1753 by Marcos Zapata. He was born in Cusco."

Unlike most paintings of the Last Supper, which are in landscape format, this one was vertical. I studied the faces of Jesus and the apostles before I worked my way down to the table. I did a double-take and erupted into laughter.

"What?" Latishia asked.

Still giggling, I asked, "Don't you see it?"

Kat covered her mouth with her hand and chuckled. "When in Peru...."

Gina put her hands on her hips and moved closer. "Well, what do you know, Jesus ate a guinea pig."

"What?" Latishia stepped closer to the painting. "I was so busy looking at the faces, I never noticed the food. Sweet Baby Jesus, you don't see that every day."

In the center of the table, a cooked intact guinea pig, minus the fur, lay paws up on a platter. Two other plates held potatoes and the ears of the large kernel corn we'd seen on our trip.

I placed my hand over my throat and swallowed. "I'm glad the chef cut the meat off the guinea pig before the waiter served it to us."

André looked surprised. "You ate guinea pig?"

We all nodded.

Latishia lifted the girls to a height that emphasized their splendor. "And alpaca, too."

Gina winked at me. "I'm not sure one tiny bite qualifies as having eaten guinea pig. I remember a good bit of talk from you about them being fluffy and cuddly pets."

Latishia planted her fists on her hips. "Does so count. He didn't ask how much I swallowed. I get credit for trying it."

Gina had her inscrutable face on. "Okay, you get partial credit."

"Partial!" Latishia's voice echoed off the walls.

Kat waved her arms like a referee calling a foul. "Enough! Have y'all forgotten we're in a church? It's pretty bad when the Buddhist in the group has to remind you Christians to behave in a cathedral."

André tried to suppress a grin while his attention ping-ponged back and forth between my friends. Looking unsure what to do next, he stepped back a few paces to observe. "You remind me of my sisters."

"How many sisters do you have?" I asked.

"Too many." He held up five fingers. "I have five bossy sisters."

Latishia's bottom lip pushed forward. She crossed her arms and glared at Gina, who gazed up at the painting, ignoring her. I've known Gina long enough to know she was trying to act innocent of wrongdoing after baiting Latishia.

"Now that Gina's had her fun, what's next?" I asked.

Gina turned and tried to stare me down. The mischievous glint in her eyes and the twitch at the corner of her mouth ruined the effect.

"Let's explore the plaza," André said, trying to hide his amusement.

We left the church and entered the plaza. The bright sun forced me to put on shades. "What a beautiful fountain," I said.

André pointed toward the top. "The statue at the top is Pachacuti, who was the ninth ruler of the Kingdom of Cusco. Later he became the Emperor of the Inca Empire."

"A man of high ambition," Kat said. "I like the white birds at the base."

"A lamb!" Latishia said.

Kat drew her brows together. "I know what a bird looks like."

"No." Latishia pointed across the square. "There's a white lamb over there." She took off at a good brisk walk.

André ran after her, with the rest of us close behind. When we caught up, Latishia wore a child-like smile while petting a lamb held in the arms of a young woman dressed in bright Peruvian garb.

This woman's hat was different than any we'd seen. The top was a large flat circle of colorful, embroidered fabric with a draping border of red fringe. Every aspect of her costume was elaborately decorated, from her jacket, to her full skirt, to her shoes.

Latishia shoved her camera at André. "I want my photo with the lady and her lamb."

André smiled and nodded to the young lady. "You must pay to take a photo with her. This is how she makes money."

"Will five dollars be enough?" I asked, digging through my purse.

He spoke to the lady in Spanish. "Sí."

Latishia had her photo done first, then we did one with all the Divas. When we finished the lamb baaed its complaint.

"I guess the little guy has had enough of us," I said. "The sun is hot, I'm tired, and my legs feel like heavy logs."

"I will take you to your hotel. It is only a short walk."

After we checked into Hotel Xima and received our room keys, we wandered into the spa.

"I think we deserve Diva massages," Gina said, rotating her shoulders to loosen them.

"I'm with you," I said. "My legs are stiffening like curing concrete. They hurt more today than they did last night. If I stand or sit too long, they don't want to bend."

After determining a price, we followed our massage therapists into separate rooms.

***

I left the massage room grateful that my legs felt like legs again, instead of water-soaked logs. I strolled past two women talking near the spa entrance.

"We're going home tomorrow. Did you hear there are now over a hundred confirmed cases of the virus?"

I paused. *What virus? Who has over a hundred cases?* I turned back to ask the ladies what they were talking about, but they'd disappeared into the spa.

***

We met in the hotel restaurant for dinner that night. We were all too tired to venture out. After massages and a wonderful meal, I felt almost human.

Yawning, I said, "I don't know about y'all, but I'm bushed."

"Lordy, I'm going to need a vacation to recover from my vacation." Latishia yawned and patted her mouth. "Somehow, I never thought our adventure would be so physical. If I'd known, I'd have done more walking to prepare."

"Best that we get to bed. We have an early pick up tomorrow," Kat said.

"I'm ready for a shower first, then bed," Gina said, running her fingers through her curls.

We trudged over to the elevator and went to our rooms.

My thought as I unlocked my room was, *I hope there are no problems with our flights home.*

CHAPTER 17: Bad News

André arrived at the hotel in the wee hours to drive us to the airport. The sun wasn't up yet and the hotel lobby was dim.

I rolled my case over to him. "Buenos días, André."

The Divas joined us.

His return greeting matched his worried look. The Divas and I exchanged glances.

"What's wrong, André?" I stifled a yawn. "Was our flight to Lima canceled?" *Please no!*

He shook his head and looked at his shoes. He took a deep breath and met my gaze. "Your flights are fine. Our office told me some bad news this morning. A person from Spain who was on tour with you in Lima was hospitalized and died."

"What!" Latishia placed a hand over her heart. "What happened?"

"Complications from a confirmed case of this new coronavirus."

Kat's mouth dropped open. She grabbed his sleeve. "The one that started in Wuhan, and spread across China?"

He nodded.

The color drained from Kat's face. She took a step back and looked at me.

I clutched the handle of my luggage tighter. "I bet it was the guy who was coughing his guts out in the back of the van."

"Sweet Baby Jesus!" Latishia looked around as if the virus was ready to attack from all directions.

Gina placed a hand on Kat's shoulder. "What should we do?"

She turned to André. "Where can we get some masks?"

He shrugged. "It's too late to find any. Besides, none of the stores are open at this hour. I was told they are taking everyone's temperature before they board overseas flights."

Kat pivoted and eyed us. "Any cold-like symptoms, aches, coughing, or fever?"

Latishia raised her hand. "Do hot flashes count?"

"No. Let's get on the van and wipe down our seats or anything we might touch. I'm calling Dr. Howard. I'll tell him what's going on and see if he can round up four testing kits. Last I heard, from first exposure to the early symptoms could be up to fourteen days."

We boarded the van and pulled out our wipes.

"This virus scares me," Kat said as she scrubbed her seatbelt buckle.

Gina looked up from wiping. "Why? Isn't it simply the flu?"

"No. There are different kinds of flu viruses. Most aren't a coronavirus."

Gina stopped cleaning.

Kat continued, "Think of the category of Coronavirus like a family tree with nineteen branches. Each of those branches is a different version of the virus. Only three of those branches have transferred from animals to humans."

"What are those three?" I asked while continuing to sanitize.

"They are MERS-CoV, SARS-CoV, and SARS-CoV-2. Each of these has high mortality rates," Kat said.

"God help us. How high?" Latishia asked.

Kat settled her glasses to a better position. "I don't remember off the top of my head, but they are killers."

"Where does this current one fit on your tree? What's it called?" I asked.

Kat wiped down her phone. "COVID-19. According to Dr. Howard, it would be a leaf on the SARS-CoV-2 branch. He was following all the reports on the virus before we left town."

André had been following our conversation. "Why does this one worry you?" he asked.

Kat wiped her forehead with the back of her wrist. "We're not completely sure how it spreads. The last I heard it was from droplets when we sneeze or cough, and from contaminated surfaces. New information comes in bits and pieces anytime there's a new contagion."

André nodded, looking more worried.

"Have y'all heard of Typhoid Mary? Before her, we didn't know people who appeared healthy could spread a disease. We could be asymptomatic spreaders and not even know it." Kat held up her phone. "I need to call Doc."

We sat and listened to her conversation. I wondered what would happen if we developed the virus. *Will we be quarantined? If so, what will that mean? Will Buffy get it?*

"I should've paid more attention to the reports about this virus before I left," Latishia said. "It was so far away that I didn't think it would bother us on our travels."

The van sped along the early dawn streets of Cusco. Mountains dotted with homes and shops surrounded us. Traffic worsened when we neared the airport.

Gina held up her long hair and fanned herself with a magazine. A bead of sweat formed on her upper lip. "Odio le vampate di calore."

Latishia grunted. "Can't you ever get upset in English?"

I chuckled. "Oh, come on, Latishia. She grouches about hating hot flashes all the time. You should know that one by now."

"I'm just saying, why can't she be grouchy in English?"

Kat disconnected her call. "Dr. Howard will contact the Health Department and get the ball rolling." She patted Gina's hand. "I have bad news. Since we left, Italy is now on lockdown. He thought you'd want to know."

Gina's eyes widened. "I still have cousins living in Sicily. What do you mean by lockdown?"

"No travel, schools and businesses are closed, and folks are being asked to stay inside. Doc said the President is considering a lockdown on international flights entering the U.S. I'm glad we're on our way home."

Latishia shook her head. "Thank the Lord that I don't live in Italy right now."

"Sorry to hear about Italy, Gina, but I'm concerned that the United States' borders will be closed before we can get home. The last thing I want to do is hang out in an airport any longer than necessary." I slapped my forehead. "Brent! He doesn't know about the situation."

Kat's brow wrinkled. "Better call him."

Gina gave me a knowing look. "Sounds like you still have feelings for the man."

I grabbed my phone. "Of course I do. Feelings don't turn on and off like a faucet. Just because marriage isn't in our future doesn't mean I'm not concerned for his wellbeing."

Brent's tone sounded wary. "I wasn't expecting a call from you."

"I have some bad news."

Silence.

"Brent? Are you there?"

"Yes. What's wrong?"

I took a deep breath to steady my nerves. "We were exposed to the new coronavirus our first day in Peru."

"How did it happen?" he asked.

A shiver ran over my body like corpse hands. "A guy from Spain was coughing on our tour bus. Our guide told us minutes ago that he, he… died."

"What should I do? Does Kat have any suggestions?"

"Buy some masks and wear them. Wash your hands often. Sanitize everything before you touch it. Oh, and use hand sanitizer."

"I'll look online for other precautions," he said.

"Good idea. Sorry about this."

"Not your fault," he said.

Kat tapped my shoulder. "Tell him about the flights."

"Oh, Kat just reminded me, the President is threatening to close the borders and not allow any international flights."

"Shit! I'm not scheduled to leave for three more days."

"Where are you?" I asked.

"I'm still in the Sacred Valley. I saw Machu Picchu yesterday. It was amazing. I understand now why your legs were so sore."

"Brent, I'd try to get out today if you can. We're about to board a plane to Lima and then home."

"I guess I'd better go." He sighed. "Lots to do. Take care of yourself. You know I still love you."

I felt a lump in my throat. "Be safe and get out of Peru, ASAP."

My eyes flooded with tears while I tucked my phone into my purse. *It's all my fault if he gets sick and stuck in Peru.*

Latishia handed me tissues from a nearby box. "What did he say?"

I blubbered, "He still loves me. I'll never forgive myself if he dies because he came to Peru to propose."

Gina rubbed circles on my back. "Now, now. We don't know if we have the virus yet. If I were you, I'd be worried he won't get home fast enough."

I wiped my eyes and remembered the Serenity Prayer that I teach my patients. I recited it in my head.

"Phoenix has a right to be concerned." Kat eyed each of us. "According to Dr. Howard, there are confirmed cases of COVID-19 across most of the United States." She looked at me. "Washington State is a hot spot."

"What about Alabama?" I asked.

She shrugged. "The state received its first testing kits at the end of last week. We really don't know yet. I suspect we do."

Gina glared. "Why are they so late to test?"

Kat held up both hands. "Don't get riled at me. Dr. Howard didn't tell me. I assume he doesn't have all the information."

The van stopped at the loading zone of the airport. André helped us out and directed us toward the rear where the driver unloaded our luggage. We took our backpacks and suitcases and followed André into the terminal.

He stopped outside the security area to answer his phone. His brown eyes widened with alarm as he looked at each of us. After a short conversation in Spanish, he ended the call. "Ladies, do not miss your flight in Lima. The Peruvian government is stopping all international flights at noon today. Your flight is one of the last to leave. If you're not on the plane and off the ground by then, you are stuck in Peru."

My stomach flipped. "There's no way Brent will make it."

"That's just great," Gina grumbled.

"André, you've been with us all week! If we're carriers, you were exposed to the virus. What will you do?" I asked.

"My office told me and all of the drivers to self-quarantine for fourteen days. They have notified all your guides and the hotels about the situation."

"Sweet Baby Jesus. Now I really do feel like Typhoid Mary," Latishia said.

"My office asked me to apologize for putting you in danger."

"It wasn't anyone's fault," Kat said.

André smiled as he handed us some tickets. "These are for your flight to Lima." He gave us another set. "These are your tickets to Dallas-Fort Worth. Don't lose them! It has been my pleasure to be your guide. I hope you have safe travels." He extended his hand.

Kat held up both of hers and stepped back. "Under the circumstances, no handshaking or hugs."

The Divas had combined assets to provide a good tip for him. I handed over a sealed envelope. "You were our best guide. Adiós."

Blushing, he accepted the tip. "Thank you."

We waved goodbye and walked over to stand in line.

My gut felt like a washer on the spin cycle. I whispered, "What if we develop a fever before we get home? What if they ask us questions about where we've been?"

Kat gave me her General Kat look. "We will take this journey one step at a time. Don't offer information. Our goal is to escape Peru and get home, where we speak the language and I feel more comfortable about the level of medical care. I'm sure we're fine because we've been careful."

I nodded, but my gut didn't believe her. I placed my items on the belt to be x-rayed and walked through the metal detector.

No response.

My shoulders slumped with relief.

Kat and Gina made it through with no problems.

We huddled to watch Latishia while she eyed the metal detector. Her chest rose and fell before she walked through.

Nothing.

Latishia gave us a thumbs up and grabbed her backpack.

I boarded the small plane with a sense of relief. This time, Kat didn't need to remind anyone to sanitize everything we'd touch.

I gazed out the window as the plane took off and wondered how Huntsville would respond to the crisis. Crossing myself, I prayed Brent would be okay.

An hour later, we landed in Lima. When we entered the terminal, Latishia hopped from foot to foot.

"I gotta go. Now!"

We reconnoitered until we found a ladies' room.

"Get outta my way," Latishia said, as she did a quick, thigh-together walk toward the ladies' room.

The rest of the Divas followed in her wake.

We entered the bathroom. Latishia chanted, "Don't pee. Don't pee. Don't pee," while pushing her way into a stall.

"Coming through," Gina said, pushing me aside.

Kat yelled like a hovering helicopter mother, "Don't touch anything!"

Ten minutes later, we were washing our hands and applying hand sanitizer.

Latishia wiped her shiny face with a paper towel. "That was close. All this tension is stressing my bladder."

We claimed our bags, which required us to leave the secured area. Once again, we made it through security with no problems.

Kat insisted we stand in a corner, away from everyone else, while we waited to board.

I checked my watch. "Only an hour until Peru shuts their borders."

The airline clerk at our gate made an announcement in Spanish. Some of the people around us groaned and conversed in rapid-fire Spanish.

Latishia looked around and frowned. "Something's wrong."

The announcement came in English. "Ladies and Gentlemen, this flight has been delayed due to a mechanical problem. We will have more information soon."

CHAPTER 18: Stressed

Latishia wrung her hands. "What're we going to do? I can't be stuck in Peru! I have a kid. He should be home from the beach by now."

I hugged her. "Calm down. We aren't stuck here, at least not yet. Sit over there, close your eyes, and pray."

She nodded rapidly. "That's a good idea."

I turned to Kat and Gina. "I wonder if there's another flight? I'm going to ask the lady who made the announcement."

The woman looked up as I approached. Her name tag had María printed on it in neat block letters.

"María, my friends and I are trying to get home to America before your country stops air traffic. Is there another flight we could take?"

Her lips thinned. "No. Everything is booked. I will give updates as I get them." She looked down at the paper in front of her and ignored me.

When I returned, Latishia had her eyes scrunched tight and her hands folded in her lap. Kat, who was seated next to her, focused on her phone.

Gina was on the move. I tapped her on the shoulder as she passed. She whirled to face me. "Any news?"

"All the flights are booked. The airline will announce an update when they know something."

Gina swallowed hard. "Walk with me. I can't sit still right now."

She shot down the concourse. I struggled to keep up.

"Is this a race or something?" I asked.

"Sorry." Gina slowed to a reasonable pace. "If we're in the middle of a pandemic, I want to be home, not in Lima."

"I agree." I linked arms with her. "I think we need some chocolate." I steered her to a nearby store.

Ten minutes later, Gina and I stood smiling in front of our friends.

Gina rattled the bag. "It's time for chocolates!"

"Hot damn!" Latishia leaped to her feet.

Kat's brows inched up her forehead. "I thought you were a pious Southern Baptist."

"These are desperate times, don't mess with me," Latishia said, her gaze glued to the bag.

Gina spilled an assortment of chocolate bars onto the table between Kat and Latishia. We fell on them like ravenous, chocolate-deprived women.

Two bars later, I felt calmer. *Must be the serotonin.*

Gina sported chocolate on her chin and was licking her fingers like a toddler. "Mmm, that hit the spot. Good idea, Phoenix." She smirked. "We got chocolate in Lima after all."

"Amen to that." Latishia had a high-on-chocolate grin on her face.

Always the mother, Kat gathered the wrappers and took them to a nearby trash can.

An announcement in Spanish boomed over the speakers. Some of the people around us smiled and clapped.

"Ladies and gentlemen, the mechanical problem on this flight is resolved. We will begin boarding in five minutes."

I looked at my watch. "We'll be cutting it close."

Gina made the sign of the cross and looked to Heaven.

Once we were on the plane, we passed through section after section to reach the very back. We were only five rows away from the toilets.

"I've forgotten," I said. "Who picked these seats?"

"Me," Kat said, pushing her glasses up with a finger. "Why?"

"We're always stuck at the back of the plane. We're the last to board and the last to get off."

Kat sighed and stopped cleaning her area. "I did some research and —"

Gina interrupted. "That doesn't surprise me."

Kat sliced a sharp glare at Gina.

Gina raised her hands. "I'm not saying that's a bad thing."

"As I was saying, research shows the passengers in the back of the plane have a higher survival rate during a crash. Besides, we all have bladders the size of a golf ball, so we need to be close to the toilets." Kat wrinkled her nose. "But not too close."

"Amen to that," Latishia said. "Sometimes I feel like the princess and the pea, only the pea is my bladder."

The flight attendant announced, "Ladies and gentlemen, we ask that you take your seats as quickly as possible."

I looked at my watch. "We only have fifteen minutes to beat the deadline to have our flight off the ground."

We settled down, secured our backpacks under the seats, and fastened our seatbelts.

I waited, praying we would make it. "Why aren't we moving?"

A few moments later, the plane taxied toward the runway.

I glanced at my watch. "Ten minutes to the deadline." My heart raced while the plane slowly joined the line of jets waiting to take off.

Latishia fumbled with her seatbelt. "I've got to go."

Kat chuckled. "This is why I made sure she has an aisle seat."

"I can't help it. Take-offs make me nervous."

Gina whispered, "You have to hold it. If you get up and stop this flight from leaving the country, the folks on this plane might line up to slap some sense into you like they did in the Airplane movie."

The flight attendant gave her a stern look. "Ma'am, fasten your seat belt."

Latishia looked miffed, but she did. She gripped the armrests and closed her eyes.

The plane sat at the end of the runway, revving its engines.

I thought, *Go. Go. Go.*

It sped down the runway, the acceleration pushing me against the seat. The wheels left the ground. I swallowed hard to clear my ears as we gained altitude.

My watch showed noon. "Phew, we made it without a minute to spare."

The instant the seatbelt sign went off, Latishia said, "Gotta go." She unbuckled and headed toward the toilet.

"Who wants to bet she'll complain about the size of the bathroom?" Gina asked.

I nudged her. "I won't take that bet. Who doesn't complain? It's worse than an RV."

Latishia lumbered back down the aisle and settled into her seat. Belted in, she looked across the aisle at Gina and me. "Lordy, if they made those restrooms any smaller, a flea couldn't turn around. I almost got stuck in there."

Gina giggled, which set off Kat and me. Once we started, we couldn't stop laughing.

"What's so funny?" Latishia asked, looking cross.

Between gasps of breath, I croaked, "Flea," before breaking into another spasm of laughter.

Latishia started to giggle. "I didn't think it was that funny."

We'd manage to get some level of control until we looked at each other. This triggered another session of the laugh fest. The people in the seats around us stared as if we were insane. Any utterance of the word "flea" would set us off again.

I wiped laughter tears from my eyes. "Now I have to visit one of those tiny rooms."

"Me, too," Gina said, standing.

When we returned, I scooted into my window seat. "Boy, I can tell the tension is running high when I lose it over the word 'flea.' We needed a good laugh."

Gina sat next to me and tittered. "Stop, don't make me start again."

A woman two rows up headed toward the toilet, fumigating us with a cloud of sweet-smelling perfume. *Glad I'm not sitting next to her.*

Latishia scrunched her nose, sneezed, and waved her hand in front of her face.

"Good grief, did she marinate in that scent overnight?" Gina whispered.

When she came past again on the way to her seat, Gina had her magazine out, fanning for all she was worth.

Kat coughed and leaned over to see past Latishia. "Stop sending it this way. Do you want me to choke to death?"

Another odor, definitely not floral, filled the air. Rancid came to mind.

Latishia scrunched her nose again. "Did something die?"

"Fan faster," I said.

The man sitting in front of Gina stood and headed toward the restrooms.

Gina fanned with all her might. "This is going to be a long flight. Glad I went to the restroom before he did."

I can't wait to get off this plane. To distract myself, I asked, "What have y'all missed the most while we were gone?"

Kat smiled and counted on her fingers. "Jack, my parents, and my bed. There's no bed like your own."

Latishia looked up and tapped her lips with a finger. "Dante, Aaron, my parents, and my shower. It seemed like most of the showers were too weak. What about you, Gina?"

"I agree with the bed and shower. As zany as my family can be, I really miss them. I would kill for some of my Mom's lasagna right now."

They all looked at me. "Buffy, my home, and Mike."

Gina nudged me with a sly smile. "You don't miss Brent?"

"Not as much since we broke up. Since we parted at the hotel, I've been trying to emotionally distance myself. It's hard because I'm concerned that he's stuck in Cusco. What if he catches the virus?"

Kat looked up from her book. "That could be a problem. The local hospital may not be equipped to handle an epidemic. The biggest concern, according to Doc, is the supply of ventilators. They're expensive, so smaller facilities may only have a few."

"I'll text Brent when we land. If he's stranded in Peru, his mother will have a meltdown of epic proportions."

Gina flipped a page of a magazine she'd found in the seat pocket. "Does he speak Spanish?"

I shrugged. "He took German in high school. Like us, he probably learned enough Spanish for travel purposes."

Gina waggled her brows at me and grinned. "Do you plan to tell Mike that Brent is out of the running?"

I thought about it a moment. "If he asks, I'll tell the truth."

Latishia frowned. "Why not tell him?"

"Two reasons. My relationship with Brent is personal and none of his business. More importantly, if he finds out, he'll increase his campaign to get married."

Latishia nodded. "That makes sense. He's used to getting his way, and the man wants you."

I closed my eyes to contemplate my situation. I wasn't looking forward to playing catch up with my business. The first week was usually a frenzy of appointments and paperwork. *Then there's Mike.* I had to admit I missed him more than Brent. *Maybe with Brent out of the picture, my feelings for Mike will become clear.*

We settled in and relaxed. When Latishia started snoring, I put on my noise-canceling headphones and plugged them in to watch a romantic comedy. I couldn't help but wonder what medical disaster loomed at home.

CHAPTER 19: Pandemic!

We arrived in Dallas-Fort Worth Airport without a hitch. All the passengers had their temperatures taken before they could exit the plane, which slowed the process to a crawl. Thank goodness our temperatures were in the normal range.

We followed the crowd to get our luggage. After we pulled our bags off the belt, Kat sanitized each handle.

She made us sanitize our hands, too. "There's no telling who's handled our luggage. I'm not taking any chances with a world-wide pandemic occurring."

I froze in place. "Pandemic! You called it an epidemic earlier. Exactly what is a pandemic?"

"It's a disease epidemic that affects most of the world," Kat said.

Latishia plopped a fist on her hip. "You didn't call it a whatchamacallit when we were in Peru."

"I didn't want to spook you, but I have a feeling when we get back to Huntsville, we're about to be bombarded with a ton of news reports about this virus," Kat said.

"True," I said. "When there's a medical crisis across the ocean, it gets a little coverage on the national evening news. When it's in America, the news coverage goes viral, no pun intended."

Kat looked worried. "Airports and planes are some of the worst places to be when dealing with a contagion. Stay away from people and don't shake hands or touch surfaces if possible. Don't touch your faces."

She swept her bangs off her brow, scratched her nose, and pushed her glasses up with a finger.

Latishia smirked. "You touched your face."

"Crap." Out came the hand sanitizer. "See how hard it is to not touch your face."

We waited in a customs line that snaked around, reminding me of a visit to Disney. At Kat's suggestion, we used our luggage to create a barrier between us and the folks in front and behind us.

Kat phoned Dr. Howard and waited while the receptionist found him. "Yes, we should be in by ten tonight. I'm going to put you on speakerphone so we can all hear you."

We crowded around to hear better.

"Ladies, the COVID-19 cases in Alabama and across the nation are increasing every day. Stay as far away from people as possible. Cover any coughs or sneezes with a tissue," Dr. Howard said.

Latishia leaned closer to the phone. "Believe me, Doc, Kat has us well in hand. If I sanitize any more, my skin may peel off."

Dr. Howard chuckled. "Good. How will you get home from the airport?"

"My parents plan to pick me up. I can't wait to see everyone," Latishia said with a huge grin.

"My brother Anthony said he'd come to get me," Gina said, before she shifted some of our luggage forward.

"My parents are picking me up, too," Kat said, tucking one side of her hair behind an ear.

"What about you, Phoenix?" he asked.

"My car is sitting in long-term parking," I said, wondering why he asked.

Dr. Howard cleared his throat. "I've explained everything to the Health Department about your exposure while on a tour bus in Lima. They want you to be tested when you arrive and to be quarantined from others."

"Quarantined!" we all said at once.

Several people around us turned with concerned looks. A few moved further away.

We huddled closer to the phone.

"I want those of you who have someone meeting you at the airport to call them and tell them not to come."

"Mama isn't going to like that at all. Aaron will like it even less," Latishia said. Her lower lip formed into a pout.

"This is a medical crisis, and we're trying to contain the spread of the virus. The elderly are at the highest risk of severe complications and death. Call whoever and tell them not to come to the airport. Get in Phoenix's car and come straight to my office. I'll test you there and send the vials to the lab. We'll know the results in two to three days at most. If the tests are negative, you can go home. If they're positive, you must stay quarantined for fourteen days."

"Fourteen days! I have a full caseload of patients for the next two weeks." I said, running my hands through my hair. "I better call my service and have them reschedule some folks."

"Where're we going to stay?" Kat asked. "My parents and Jack are at my house."

"Don't look at me. Aaron and Dante are at mine," Latishia said.

They all turned to look at me.

Gina shrugged. "I'd volunteer, but my townhome only has one spare bedroom, and it's my home office."

I held up my hands in surrender. "Y'all can stay at my place."

"Good," Doc said.

"I have a question," Gina said. "What if only one of us is positive? Do the rest get to go home?"

"You'll all be quarantined. Any more questions?"

I raised my hand, forgetting he couldn't see me. "If we were exposed six days ago, doesn't that mean we only have eight days left to quarantine?"

"No. You may be exposed to the virus at this very moment. Sorry. If your test comes back positive, you must isolate for a full fourteen days."

"Just my luck," I mumbled

"Phoenix, make a grocery and pharmacy list. Maybe some of your family can shop for you and leave the bags at your door. Buy enough for two weeks. Don't forget the hand sanitizer and sanitizing wipes," Doc said.

"I'll work with her on the list," Kat said.

"My mom and brother can get groceries. Mom may even pull some goodies from her freezer," Gina said. "Like lasagna. She usually freezes a few in case of an emergency or a funeral."

"Excellent. Don't forget to get paper goods. I'll see you later tonight," Doc said.

Kat disconnected the call and shoved the phone in her purse. "Anyone have a paper and pen?"

Gina dug through her backpack and pulled out a legal pad. Latishia produced a pen.

I leaned close to Kat and whispered, "Should we tell customs we were exposed to the virus in Lima?"

She quirked a brow. "Do you want to be quarantined here and miss our flight?"

I shook my head and made a zipping motion across my mouth.

Twenty minutes later, we made it through customs.

"Let's get something to eat and find a table so we can make a list," I said as I heaved my pack onto one shoulder. "After that, I need to call my service. It's going to be a long night."

We ordered a large pizza. While we waited, we discussed what to put on the list and watched folks rush past pulling their luggage. The airport was busy and loud. The individual conversations and public address announcements bounced off the hard surfaces, creating a deafening din.

I shoved the paper and pen in Kat's direction. "You have the neatest writing."

Gina pulled several napkins from the dispenser. "Phoenix, what do you already have on hand?"

"Not much. I tried to empty the fridge before leaving for Peru. I'm sure I have a full box of tea bags, but only one pound of coffee, so coffee should go on the list. There's plenty of flour and sugar. I bought a large bag of rice before I left."

We all started naming items to put on the list.

"Slow down! I can't write that fast," Kat said, pushing her glasses back in position.

Our steaming pizza arrived, so we put away the list to eat. The savory smell of the onions and pepperoni made my mouth water.

"Not bad," I said.

Gina scrunched her face and chewed. "For airport food."

Latishia looked over the top of her slice. "Pizza snob! At this point, I'd eat just about anything." She took a large bite and waved her hand in front of her mouth. "Hot!" She snatched her Diet Coke and gulped. She wiped her mouth and said, "Add Diet Coke to the list. I don't want to go into withdrawals."

Kat smirked and reached for another slice. She didn't drink sodas and thought they were unhealthy. "This would be a good time to stop drinking them."

Latishia scowled at Kat. "You want me to detox from Diet Coke while we're quarantined during a pandemic?" She pointed her slice of pizza at Kat. "I'll stop drinking sodas if you'll stop drinking tea."

"Whoa! Low blow," I said, looking at Kat. "Are you taking that challenge?"

Gina gesticulated in true Italian fashion. "I'm not staying with y'all if you're going to be cranky from withdrawals. Kat, please put Diet Coke on the list."

After we finished the pizza and the list, my friends made calls to their families and bosses. I called my brother, Kevin. He lives over a thousand miles away, but I didn't want him to worry. We'd become closer after our parents' deaths.

"Kevin, I'm at Dallas-Fort Worth Airport."

"Thank God. The news reported Peru planned to shut down all flights."

"We barely made it out. I haven't seen the news. Is it bad in New York?" Kevin had accepted a position there a year earlier. My nieces still live in the Chicago suburbs.

He cleared his throat. "I'm working from home. It's scary up here, so I'm self-isolating."

"Good idea." I told him about the Divas' exposure in Lima.

"I'm glad you're getting tested. Let me know the results."

We shared a bit more information and signed off.

Next I phoned the answering service.

Joni answered in her usual pert yet professional way. "Dr. O'Leary, how was Peru?"

"Absolutely beautiful. It's a trip I'll never forget."

"My husband wants to go someday. When we can manage it, I'll call you to ask what to see."

"Good idea. There is one complication, so I need your help." I explained the entire situation.

"Oh, my. How many days do we need to cancel?"

"Three. By then, I should have an answer regarding our status. If any of us test positive, we'll be quarantined for fourteen days, and we may have to take a second test."

"I sure hope that's not the case. What do I tell your patients? Folks around here are already freaking out."

"Tell them travel issues are delaying my return to the office."

"Okay. We'll start calling folks now. Good luck," Joni said.

My next call was to my next-door neighbor, Gladys. She was doggie-sitting Buffy.

"Are you home yet?" Gladys, a spry seventy-two-year-old, loves my dog almost as much as her terrier mix, Ratsy. He and Buffy are doggie buddies.

"Not yet. I hope to be there at eleven o'clock. I have a favor to ask." I explained the situation.

"Bless your heart! I bought three extra bags of dog food, thinking you might need some when you got back. I'll take a full bag over when I drop off Buffy and make sure she has plenty of food and water since you're getting home so late."

I released a sigh. "Thank you so much. I'll pay you for the food when I'm cleared."

"No, you won't, after what you've done for me over the years. It's my pleasure. Think of it as a pandemic gift."

"Thanks again."

I looked at the rest of the Divas, who were disconnecting calls. "I've handled my stuff. What about y'all?"

"I emailed Mom the grocery list. She'll deliver the groceries around eleven. Anthony will leave them on your front porch. Needless to say, she's anxious. No telling how many rosaries she'll pray before this mess is over."

"When we test negative, will you stay at your place or go over to your parents?" I asked.

"Jesus, Mary, and Joseph! Do you want me to go nuts? You know how my mother hovers. I'd gain twenty pounds in a month if I stay with them."

True. Mrs. Bongiorno thinks food is as effective as tranquilizers, antidepressants, and antibiotics combined.

"I have good news." Latishia's smile widened. "Mama will drop off some homemade goodies the day after tomorrow and wave at us."

"That's great," I said. "I hope Willy will barbecue some ribs, and Mama Snide will make macaroni and cheese."

Gina looked heavenward. "From your mouth to God's ears."

"My parents plan to do the same. Maybe I should ask them to wait a couple of days before bringing Chinese food. The way it sounds, we won't starve." Kat wiped her glasses with a napkin. "Mom sounded so worried. I don't think they'll feel at ease until they can see I'm not sick."

The loudspeaker announced our flight. We headed toward the gate and kept our distance from others. While waiting to board, I thought, *Wonder what kind of test this will be?*

CHAPTER 20: Almost Home

My heart swelled with relief when I saw the Huntsville airport out the plane's window.

Gina nudged me with her elbow. "I wonder how long this testing will take. I'm exhausted."

I frowned at her. "If you don't stop poking me, I'm going to perform an elbowectomy."

She grinned and jabbed me again.

Sighing in resignation, I said, "Shouldn't take long. I'm impressed that Dr. Howard is meeting us this late at his office."

"He probably wouldn't go to this much trouble if it wasn't for Kat. I'm sure he needs her back at work," Gina said, stuffing a small book into her backpack.

We gathered our things and worked our way to the front of the plane. "Be our luck the luggage will still be in Dallas-Fort Worth," I said.

Kat looked over her shoulder. "Don't jinx us. For three of us, the clothes in our luggage are all we have to wear."

We walked away from the gate into an almost deserted airport. A busy one is maddening, but an empty one is spooky, especially at night.

Latishia looked around. "Where is everybody?"

I shrugged. "Don't know." Our voices eerily reverberated in the space.

We followed the people ahead of us to the baggage claim area. People stood around, wilting on their feet. A light flashed, followed by a deafening beep, and the conveyor started moving.

Suitcase, please show up. I'm not sure I can take anymore. Tears welled in my eyes. Swiping them away, I told myself, *It's okay, I'm just exhausted. Things will look better after a good night's sleep.*

Latishia lunged forward. "There's mine."

Once we had them all, Kat pulled out the wipes and gave them to me. "Sanitize every surface. We don't want to contaminate your car." She slipped her phone from her fanny pack and alerted Dr. Howard to our ETA.

We pulled our bags outside, across the street, and into the long-term parking garage. The buzzing fluorescent lights cast creepy shadows among the vehicles in this manmade concrete cavern. Images of muggers, rapists, and evil incarnate flitted along the edges of my vision.

Icy fingers of alarm traced down my back. *Thank goodness I'm not in here alone.*

After two packing attempts and one zinger of an Italian temper tantrum, we managed to shove four large suitcases, four backpacks, and four Divas into my Prius.

Interstate 565 seemed deserted. I turned onto Memorial Parkway and headed south.

"There's usually more traffic at this time of night," Gina said.

I took the Drake Avenue exit. Five minutes later, I pulled into the parking lot of Dr. Howard's office.

"It looks different at night," Kat said.

We piled out of the car and walked toward the front door.

Latishia was the first to reach the door. She shrieked and scrambled back. "Sweet Baby Jesus!" She held both hands over her chest like she was trying to keep her heart inside. "I thought he was a haint."

Dr. Howard, clothed in a gown, face shield, mask, and gloves, unlocked the door.

"I didn't mean to scare you. I'm Dr. Howard. You must be Latishia since these other ladies are my patients."

"I live in Decatur, so I see Dr. Brown."

Doc nodded. "I know Mark. I'll let him know what's going on and make sure he gets a copy of your test results." He waved a purple-gloved hand. "Please don't touch anything and follow me." We squeezed into an examination room. Doc had the tests laid out with the labels ready.

"Who wants to go first?"

Kat raised her hand. "I will. Let's get this over with."

Doc took the longest swab I've ever seen and stuck it up her nose. Her face scrunched with discomfort.

"Sorry, I have to go deep to get a good sample. The Health Department trained me yesterday when I picked up the kits," he said.

Latishia took a step back, looking alarmed. "Good Lord, he's about to do brain surgery."

Kat quirked a smile at her and said, "That's what it felt like."

Gina went next. The minute Doc came at her with the swab, she screwed her eyes shut and mumbled a Hail Mary. When he finished, she blinked several times. "Ow!"

I gestured for Latishia to go next. She shook her head.

I leaned my head back and said, "Be gentle."

"I'll do my best."

I stiffened when he came at me with the swab. The sensation of pressure hurt. After he withdrew the swab, I scrunched my nose a few times trying to stop the pain.

We advanced on Latishia while Doc prepared my sample for shipping. She looked ready to bolt out the door.

"Your turn," I said.

Kat and Gina each grabbed an arm and held on. We knew from past history that Latishia had fainted numerous times while receiving injections. When Doc approached her, she leaned away.

"Tilt your head back, so I have better access," Doc said, with a reassuring tone.

When the swab came toward her, Latishia's eyes widened and focused in, making her look cross-eyed. Her chest heaved as she gulped air.

She's hyperventilating. If Doc doesn't finish soon, she's going to have a panic attack.

When he finished, Latishia went limp. Kat and Gina struggled to hold her up.

I stepped forward and patted her cheek. "You're fine. Take some deep breaths."

Doc stepped away. "All done. You might want to let her sit a minute. I'll call Kat as soon as I know something. Meanwhile, y'all are quarantined inside Phoenix's house."

"Can we go outside in my fenced backyard?" I asked.

"Only if no one else is around."

We took that moment to thank him for the medications he prescribed for our trip. Gina and I hefted Latishia to her feet and left.

Once we were back in my car, I said, "Looks like another Diva sleepover."

CHAPTER 21: The Quarantine Begins

We trudged through the garage door into my kitchen. Buffy exploded into the room, yipping and prancing around as she greeted one Diva, then another. My fog of despair evaporated as we attempted to pet whatever part of my squirming pooch came into reach.

Gina smiled and stood straight. "Nothing like being welcomed home by a dog. Maybe I should get one."

"I think that's a great idea," Latishia said from a squat as she rubbed Buffy's ears.

Kat wiped her glasses on her shirttail. "A cat might be easier. You loved the two you had before."

Gina's eyes misted with tears. "I still miss Jasmine and Oscar. I should've put them in my bedroom during the sofa delivery. If I had, they would still be with me." She looked down.

I patted her shoulder. "If I remember correctly, Oscar was an escape artist. Knowing his ability to open your door handles, it may not have made a difference. Why do you want to switch to a dog?"

"A litter box isn't my thing. I hated cleaning the stinky thing. Besides, I need a pet that's a bit more demonstrative. I need a snuggle bunny, like Buffy."

I placed my purse on the counter. "If you get a puppy, you'll have to train it to go outside."

"True. I've been thinking about this for a while. I can put a dog access in the door to my walled-in garden area that leads to my double garage. There's a grassed area, a small flower bed, and my patio where my table and four chairs sit."

I nodded. "You'd have to poopy scoop often, and the puppy would still need walks."

"A good excuse to get some exercise. The area is small, so it shouldn't be a problem," Gina said.

I yawned. "Sounds like you have it worked out. When will your brother deliver the groceries?"

Gina looked at her watch. "In thirty minutes or so."

I clapped a few times to get the others' attention. "Let's get organized before the groceries arrive. Kat, you have the lovely daybed in my office. Latishia, you have the guest room."

"Where do I sleep?" Gina asked.

"You can share my king-sized bed or sleep on the couch."

"I'll take the bed."

Kat raised a hand. "If one of us is positive, Latishia's room will become the isolation room."

I nodded. "Since that's settled, let's get our luggage in from the car. Clean clothes can go in the drawers and closets."

"Some of my things need washing," Gina said.

"I'm sure we all have dirty clothes. Put your darks in the washer. Light clothes can be piled in the laundry basket," I said. "When we get that done, we can make the beds with fresh linens."

We took off to complete our tasks. After making the beds, we collapsed onto our usual perches in the living room.

"Since we aren't going anywhere tomorrow, can we sleep in?" Latishia said in her best little girl voice.

"Okay by me. I'm beyond spent," I said, stifling a yawn. "Tomorrow, we need to get organized."

Before anyone could comment, the doorbell rang. Buffy sprinted toward the door, creating a general ruckus.

I headed for the foyer, picked up my pup, and carried her to my bedroom. After closing the door, I walked back to the living room.

Kat stood on tiptoe with her eye at the peephole. "All clear." She opened the door and walked onto the porch. We all followed.

Antonio's van idled on my driveway. He tooted his horn and turned on the interior light, so we could see him and Gina's mom waving.

We spilled out onto the sidewalk, waved manically back at them, and yelled, "Thank you." Gina threw air kisses.

The cool breeze smelled of impending rain, and the street lights had fog circles. All the houses nearby were dark.

They tooted again, pulled out of the drive, and disappeared down the street.

We hauled in plastic bags of groceries and a cooler.

We were busy putting everything away when Gina pulled the top off the cooler. "Woohoo! Mom sent a large dish of frozen lasagna." She placed it on the counter, along with a loaf of Italian bread. She reached in for another casserole dish. "This one is full of stuffed ravioli." She held up a plastic container. "Yum, minestrone soup."

I closed a cabinet door. "If we're only here a few days, I'm staking a claim on the leftovers."

"That sounds fair," Gina said.

"After you unload it, please put the cooler in the garage." I yawned again. "I'm about to fall asleep on my feet. Let's go to bed. No telling what tomorrow will bring."

CHAPTER 22: A Surprise Visit

I woke at eight-thirty, two hours later than usual. The minute my feet hit the floor, Buffy scooted into the bedroom, tail wagging with enthusiasm.

I smiled. "I'm coming, girl. Give me a minute." I followed her to the kitchen, where she stopped by her food bowl. She peered up at me with a doggie smile.

I gave her a scoop of dry food and refilled her water bowl.

"Now, it's time for me." Since there were three coffee drinkers, I readied my drip coffee maker and turned it on. Within minutes, the elixir of vitality filled the kitchen with the glorious scent of java. I located my electric teapot hidden away in a cabinet and filled it with water before plugging it in. I had the fridge door open, deliberating the breakfast choices, when Gina walked into the kitchen. Her long curls were a riotous mass this morning.

I closed the door, leaned against the counter, and said, "Good morning, Medusa."

Gina tried to pat down her hair. "Is it that bad?"

"Oh, yeah," Kat said, heading straight to the cabinet that held the tea bags.

The three of us were holding cups of our favorite brew when Latishia wandered in wearing her famous leopard pajamas. Yawning, she blinked several times before focusing in on us. She stared open-mouthed at Gina. "Was there an electrical storm this morning?"

Gina flounced off in a huff. Several minutes later, she returned with her hair constrained by a scrunchy. "There! Are y'all happy now?"

I grinned. "I was happy before." I winked at Kat. "Were you happy?"

Kat winked back. "Ecstatic."

Ignoring our shenanigans, Latishia rubbed her hands together and smiled. "What's for breakfast?"

I carried my coffee over to the table and sat. We'd had two previous Divas weekends at my home. During those, I treated my friends like houseguests. This situation was different, so I felt the need to establish some ground rules.

"Let's sit and talk about how we're going to handle the household duties during our quarantine. I don't plan to treat you like houseguests for up to fourteen days."

Kat joined me at the table with her mug of tea. "Can't blame you."

"Good," I said, patting her hand. "I vote for you to be in charge of sanitation and all medical matters."

"Works for me. I'm the obvious choice, and damn good at it."

"I think all of us need to participate in food preparation and clean up. We can do it as individuals or teams," I said.

Gina, who sat to my left, raised her hand. "I vote teams."

We all agreed on teams with Kat and me on one, and Gina and Latishia on the other. Whatever duo cooked, didn't have to clean up.

I took a sip and set down my cocker spaniel mug. "I'll wash and dry the clothes since I'm familiar with the machines, but each of us must hang and fold our clothes. Your moms don't live here."

"Deal," the three said together.

"Latishia, will you take charge of entertainment?" I asked.

She smiled. "I'm good at entertaining."

"Excellent. You know where I keep the puzzles, games, and movies. Some of us may need to do some work from home, so you don't need to worry about a twelve-hour schedule," I said.

Gina pushed a stray curl behind her ear. "What about me?"

I winked at her. "You're in charge of setting up a happy hour with snacks."

She beamed back at me. "You know my talents so well. This could be fun. No need to suffer, right?"

I raised my mug. "Hardship is a given. Suffering is optional." I stifled a yawn before taking another sip of my go-go concoction. "Do we want a big breakfast or cereal?"

Since it was so late, everyone but Latishia voted for cereal.

"If Kat agrees, we'll go first," I said.

Kat gave a thumbs up. "Fine by me."

Kat and I gathered together the cereal, milk, bananas, bowls, and other necessities.

Intrigued, I watched my friends prepare their breakfast cereals. Kat, a purist, only put the healthiest cereal in her bowl and placed her banana to the side for later.

Latishia replaced the bowl she'd received with a larger one and poured some of all four cereal choices into it. After slicing her banana on top, she drowned it with milk.

Gina read the ingredients on all the boxes before choosing two for breakfast. I suspected she was calculating the carbs since she was trying to lose twenty pounds. She skipped the banana.

Latishia eyed her banana with obvious ravenous intent. "You gonna eat that?"

Gina, whose mouth was full to chipmunk capacity, shook her head.

Latishia reached across the table and nabbed it. When she noticed us staring, she said, "Breakfast is the most important meal of the day."

We lounged around the table in our pajamas, enjoying our second round of hot beverages. I was full to the gills with milk, fiber, and fruit. After such a hectic week of travel, we deserved a relaxing day.

The doorbell rang.

Our eyes widened as we exchanged questioning looks.

Buffy banged through the rear dog door, causing us all to jump, and raced through the kitchen. She slid across the tiles and scrambled, claws digging into the living room carpet, toward the front door.

Gina's hands flew to her hair before she looked down at her pink and black polka dot pajamas. "Merda! Who could it be at this hour?"

Kat sprang to her feet and said, "Remember, we're on quarantine," before rushing to the door. She stood on tiptoes to see out the peephole. Lowering to her heels, she sighed and looked at me. "It's Mike. He's holding a large bouquet of red roses."

"What?" I shot from my chair and hustled into my bedroom. In a tizzy, I yanked off my sleepwear and tossed it on the bed. I raced to my closet, in a panic about what to wear. Huffing a bit, I snatched a pair of jeans off a hanger and hopped on one foot while jamming the other into one of the legs.

Kat yelled, "Just a minute, Mike."

"Good grief," I mumbled while trying to pull up the zipper. That completed, I pawed through my underwear drawer until I found a bra. My trembling fingers fumbled with the closure. I unsuccessfully tried to snatch a blue flannel shirt off the rack. I cursed under my breath while trying to untangle the hanger from its neighbor. Giving up, I unbuttoned it and slipped it off. I fastened it on the way to the bathroom. Once there, I stared at my hair in the mirror with a rattled expression. I brushed it and pulled it back with a scrunchy. With no time for complete makeup, I colored my lips with a nearby tube of lipstick.

Inhaling deeply, I looked in the mirror to prepare myself for the encounter. It was then I noticed my shirt was buttoned askew. I corrected the problem.

I told myself, "You can handle this, Phoenix." With erect posture and a faked outward calm, I walked out of the bedroom toward the door. Memories of our last encounter flashed through my mind.

Kat held up her hand. "You can't open the door unless he stands six feet away."

"Good grief! Where's my phone?" I used my Apple watch to ping my phone, which was on the charger in the kitchen. I retrieved it and called Mike.

"Phoenix? What the hell is going on? Why is Kat there, and why won't she let me in?" Mike asked.

I pulled the curtain aside so we could see each other. "We're quarantined."

"What!" He looked ready to charge the door. "Are you okay?"

I winced and held the phone away from my ear. "Stop yelling, and I'll explain. We have two options, talk this way or outside, but only if you agree to stay at least six feet away from me."

Silence.

He ran his hand over his face and frowned. "Come outside. That way, we'll have a little privacy from Kat."

I ended the call and opened the door. A fresh spring breeze blew loose tendrils of hair across my face. I pushed them aside. The sweet smell of my neighbor's jasmine made me smile.

Mike rushed forward two steps.

I held up a hand. "Back up."

He backed away a few feet.

"More." I made shooing motions with my hands.

When he was far enough away, I stepped out from the porch to the sidewalk. I raised my face to the sun enjoying the warmth.

The door closed behind me. I looked over my shoulder and caught the twitch of a curtain in Latishia's room.

"I brought you flowers." He smiled, using his dimples to his best advantage. He held out the roses.

His dark hair blew in the breeze, and I could tell by his deep tan he'd been on the golf course while I was gone. He looked good. I felt a tingle of desire and wanted to rush into his arms and kiss him, among other things. Then, I remembered his temper tantrum.

"Thank you, they're lovely. Please lay the bouquet on the pavement and back away. I'll give the flowers to Kat to place in a vase with water."

Mike's mouth thinned. I could tell he didn't like it, but he placed them on the sidewalk and backed up.

The situation wasn't ideal, but I couldn't risk infecting him. "Further away."

When he was at a safe distance, I picked up the bouquet and inhaled the blooms' sweet aroma. "Wonderful. This will help to cheer us." I turned and walked to the door and knocked.

Kat opened it and took the roses.

I walked back to where I'd been.

"Phoenix, what in Sam Hill is going on? I show up with flowers, and instead of a kiss and hug from you, Kat yells for me to wait at the door. Then it took forever for you to show up." He adopted a chin up, arms crossed pose.

Yep, he's upset. I crossed my arms and cocked a hip. "If you'd calm down, I'll explain. We were still in our pajamas, for christsakes. We didn't get to bed until after midnight. I had to get dressed."

"Oh, sorry about that." His chin lowered. "I forgot your flight arrived late."

Starting with the bus tour in Lima, I told the story of our current quarantined status. Several of my neighbors gave us curious looks as they drove by. I gave each one a cheery wave and continued my explanation. "That's why the four of us are staying at my house until our test results come in."

"I appreciate you keeping your distance under these circumstances. Rachael and the baby are staying with me for a bit. I'll explain it all later. I think it's just another flu, but Rachael isn't sure how this whole pandemic will work out." He ran both hands through his thick dark hair. "The reported cases of this virus are on the rise everywhere. Even worse, the stock market is dropping like a skydiving elephant without a parachute."

The stock market dropping is worse than people dying? "Crazy times. Let's keep in touch by phone or FaceTime."

He took a step forward with open arms, stopped, and dropped them to his sides.

I blew him a kiss.

He pantomimed catching it.

"I really do love the roses. Stay safe and healthy. Tell Rachael I said hello." I waved and walked inside.

My friends sprinted toward the living room. When they spotted me, they froze in place with guilty looks.

"Are we playing Freeze Tag?" I managed my best "ticked off" expression. "I guess I don't have to tell you anything, since y'all heard and watched it all."

They had the decency to look contrite.

"Not quite all of it," Gina said. "Kat kept trying to shoo us away from the window."

"I could use another cup of coffee." I left them exchanging embarrassed looks, all except Gina. She wore a smirky grin.

CHAPTER 23: Paper Crisis

Gina and Latishia were doing breakfast cleanup when my Apple watch pinged. The screen read, *Madison County COVID-19 task force to give a briefing.*

I turned on the television to Channel 48, where our handsome mayor sat behind a microphone. "Y'all come listen."

I sat in my recliner and pulled up the footrest. My friends sat in their usual places. The more I heard, the more frightened I became.

Latishia's eyes were round as Frisbees. "They're shutting down restaurants, except for take-out?"

"Sounds like it," I said.

Gina's hand covered her mouth while staring at the television. She looked over at me. "They've closed the courts. I need to call my secretary." Standing, she headed toward the bedroom and closed the door.

When the report ended, I stood and rubbed my temples. I needed a bit of normalcy. "I'm going to start the washer. If you have whites, get them in there now."

I wasn't keen to do the clothes, but I needed a distraction to keep my mind off the world's turmoil. I was doing my best to reframe the current situation to a positive one when Gina walked into the living room, holding an empty cardboard roll.

"Phoenix, where do you keep the spare toilet paper?"

"Under the sink."

"I looked," Gina said. "I didn't see any."

I rolled my eyes and walked to the master bath, mumbling, "I'm sure there's some in here. It was on the list." I yanked open the door and peeked inside.

No paper.

I dropped to my knees, so I could see into the back corner.

None.

I checked the other side of the cabinet.

Nothing.

Using the counter, I pulled myself to my feet and rushed into the guest bath to look inside the cabinet under the sink.

One roll.

"Did you find any?" Gina asked.

I handed her the roll. "That's the last one."

Her eyes popped wide. "It can't be. Wasn't it on the grocery list?"

We rushed toward the kitchen.

Kat stood at the counter dunking her tea bag into a mug. The looks on our faces caused her to do a double-take. "What's wrong?"

"Did you see any toilet paper when we put away the groceries last night?" I asked.

Her brows furrowed. "Not that I remember. Why?"

Holding the empty cardboard roll for her to see, I said, "We have one and a half rolls to last for the next three days."

Latishia lumbered into the room. "No way! For four women with overactive bladders?"

Gina picked up her phone. "Nonna, let me speak to Mom." She waited, tapping her foot. "Mom, did you forget to buy toilet paper?" Her eyes widened. "You're kidding." She listened intently. "Okay. Love y'all."

She put the phone into her jeans pocket. "Mom said the store shelves were empty of all paper products. Kroger is due to get a shipment in two days. Mom will go back then and try to get some for us."

I held my head between my hands and tried to think. "Don't panic." I stood on tiptoe to peer at the shelf above the washer. It whirled into a spin cycle, vibrating the machine. The faint odor of bleach hung in the air.

"We have an unopened pack of napkins and six rolls of paper towels." I turned to face my friends. "If we need to, we're going to cut the paper towels into the appropriate sizes and throw them in the trash after use."

Latishia did her neck thing. "It's like being in Peru again."

I scowled at her. "We have no choice. My septic system isn't designed to flush and process paper towels. I don't want to have to call a plumber."

Latishia cast her gaze to the floor. "Sorry. I didn't think about the septic system."

Kat shook her head. "This is crazy! Stuff like this doesn't happen during a winter storm, and this city practically shuts down when it snows."

Gina looked worried. "Mom told me the canned vegetable and meat sections were almost empty, and the sanitizing wipes were gone."

Kat turned toward me. "We need to check your cleaning supplies. I don't remember seeing any of those, either, when we put away the groceries."

"I was so beat last night that I don't remember half of what I did," I admitted.

The final count was one Lysol disinfectant spray, one full container of Clorox wipes, the usual array of cleaning supplies, and a large pump bottle of Purell with Aloe.

Kat held up the Purell. "We can all fill our personal bottles from this one. Did anyone check our supply of soap?"

"Mom said the soap was wiped out, too. She did manage to get the last eggs."

Latishia raised her hand and grinned. "I saved all those sample soaps from the hotels."

Kat high-fived Latishia. "Those may come in handy. Phoenix, where do you keep your soap supply?"

"In the bathrooms, under the sinks."

Kat strode in that direction with her arms pumping.

Gina crossed her arms. "General Kat is in woman on a mission mode."

"I heard that," Kat said.

When she returned, she reported, "Two extra bars under each sink. That's good because there's going to be a whole lot of hand-washing."

We sat in the living room, trying to digest what we'd discovered today.

Kat removed her glasses and rubbed both eyes. "I've been researching this on the computer. It's bad. New York, New Jersey, and Washington State are in crisis. From the projections I saw, Alabama is maybe three weeks behind the surge."

The impact hit me like a hammer to the solar plexus. I struggled to catch my breath. "If we have COVID-19, how many people did we infect along the way?"

Kat put her glasses back on and hung her head. "I don't even want to think about it. My focus was on keeping us healthy. I only hope the measures we took on the bus were enough."

Gina's hand covered her heart. "So many folks. Think about it, our guides and drivers, the hotel staff, the waiters—"

Latishia interrupted. "The people on the train and in the shops."

"We could've transported the virus across much of Peru." I sat straighter. "I need to contact Brent."

CHAPTER 24: Stuck

Once I was in my bedroom with the door closed, I texted Brent. *Did you get out?*

He texted back, *Call me.*

When I phoned, he asked, "Did you get home?"

"Yes. The bad news is, the Divas and I are quarantined at my house until our COVID-19 test results come in."

"When will that be?"

"Hopefully, in a couple of days. I'll let you know the outcome, "I said, feeling guilt-ridden.

"I took off for Cusco shortly after we talked. I was walking into the airport when someone told me Peru stopped the oversea flights," he said.

"I'm so sorry. Are you still in Cusco?"

"No, I made it to Lima. Cusco was a bit too primitive for me. If I get ill, I want a modern facility with respirators. I phoned my parents with the bad news. Mom is about to have a fall-apart."

Not wanting to comment on his mother's mental state, I said, "I don't blame you for going to Lima. I thought we would be stuck there, too. Our flight had a mechanical problem that delayed our takeoff. We left the ground exactly at noon."

"I'm glad y'all made it. Mom and Dad are back home and quarantined until they get their test results."

I sucked in a breath. "What happened?"

"You may have heard on the news that the state of Washington is a hot spot for the virus. Their realtor tested positive and contacted them at home."

"Crap." A chill ran over me when I thought about Mr. Powers' previous heart attack. "Your dad is in the high-risk category for severe symptoms."

"Yeah. That, along with me stuck in Peru, has Mom on the edge of collapse." There was a long pause. "Phoenix, would you go check on them? They don't live far from you."

I shook my head. "I'm quarantined. Remember?"

"Maybe if you called them —"

I interrupted him. "Have you told them I turned down your proposal?"

There was a long hesitation. "Well, yeah."

I shook my head again. "Sorry, no way. She'll verbally eviscerate me."

He sighed. "You're right. That's not such a good idea."

Relieved, I said, "Let me know when you get home."

"Will do. Phoenix, I —."

"Please, don't say it."

I disconnected the call, stood, and took a few deep breaths. Buffy sat at my feet, looking up at me. When I opened the bedroom door and stepped out, the Divas stood in a semicircle looking at me.

"What did he say?" Gina asked, pulling her hair out of the bun. It tumbled across her shoulders.

"Did he make it out of Peru?" Latishia asked, one hand fisted on her hip.

I held up both hands. "Nosy! Nosy!" I shared the highlights of our conversation.

Kat gave a feline stretch. "I'm glad he's in Lima. The hospitals will be better equipped."

Latishia did her neck thing. "I can't believe he asked you to call his parents."

"Me, either. We need some entertainment. Latishia, why don't you pick out a romantic comedy? I'll make some popcorn."

CHAPTER 25: Food Heaven

The smell of Mama Bongiorno's homemade lasagna filled the house. Gina and Latishia were in charge of this meal, since lunch was popcorn and a movie.

Gina had constructed an antipasto plate of cubed mozzarella, salami slices, and black olives served with a bottle of Chianti. We settled into the living room to 'happy hour' our way through the horrendous events on the evening news.

"This is terrible! Italy is almost decimated by this virus." Gina gulped some of her wine. "Mom called some of our relatives. So far, everyone's well."

"That's good news." Latishia popped a cube of cheese into her mouth. She chewed a moment and spoke. "Mama said her sister in Detroit tested positive and is quarantined at home. She's worried and feels helpless since she can't go take care of her."

"I know it's hard. Mama Snide is such a nurturer. I'm praying Kevin and my nieces are staying isolated." I took a sip of wine. "Chicago and New York have high infection rates."

Kat nodded. "I don't know about y'all, but I feel like we're characters in a science fiction movie."

Latishia did her neck thing. "If that's the case, I demand the lead role."

Gina rolled her eyes. "Not." She flipped her hair over her shoulder and struck a sexy pose. "This clearly calls for an Italian sex goddess."

Latishia harrumphed. "Sex goddess my ass."

Kat shook her head and looked my way. "Phoenix, why did your family move up north?"

I shrugged. "Kevin found himself suddenly unemployed, so he went where the jobs were."

Gina stuck her feet into her fuzzy pink slippers and stood. "Who wants the last olive?"

Kat reached over and nabbed it.

Gina picked up the plate. "Okay Latishia, we have salad and garlic bread to make."

Kat grabbed her phone. "I'm going to call the folks."

"Good idea. I'll call Mike." I went to my bedroom and closed the door.

"How's the quarantine going?" Mike asked.

"Good and bad."

"Let's get the bad out of the way first."

I sighed. "We're low on toilet paper."

"That's a bummer." He chuckled.

I huffed and glared at the phone. "It's not funny. Four women with menopausal bladders, stuck in one house with a half-roll of TP per restroom, is a crisis in the making."

"I thought you'd be one of those women who'd stock up on things."

Trying to keep annoyance out of my voice, I said, "Normally, yes. Remember, I was on vacation, so I let supplies dwindle. I typically stock up when I return."

"Makes sense. This coronavirus mess seems to have hit so quickly."

"I thought so, too, until I caught up on the news. It appears the government was warned in January and pooh-poohed the whole thing. The President didn't take it seriously until the nation was in a mess."

Mike had voted for the President. Sounding gruff, he said, "Let's not argue politics."

I stared at the phone and took a deep breath before replying. "First, I'm not arguing. Second, I'm discussing preparedness for a medical and social crisis resulting in many deaths, among other things."

Silence.

"Mike, we're all pretty overwhelmed by the enormity of the situation."

"Why? It's been all over the news."

I blew a strand of hair out of my face. "Before our trip, we made a pact to stay off our phones, except for texts with family and friends. We never watched the news in Peru because it was in Spanish." I paused to let that sink in. "Mike, we were ignorant about the world crumbling around us. The last we'd heard, China had a flu epidemic in one area. Imagine our surprise when our tour guide informed us, right before we left Cusco, that we'd been exposed to COVID-19 on our first day in Lima. We were doing our best to process the implications when he received the call that we had until noon to get out of Peru."

He grunted. "I didn't think about all the local news being in Spanish. To be truthful, I haven't watched much news, except about the stock market." He paused. "I'm worried about Rachael. It's struck her hard. I've had to limit her to one newscast a day. She sat in front of the TV for three days straight, flipping from news report to news report. Poor kid couldn't sleep from worrying."

The happy clatter of dishes and the closing of cabinet doors alerted me that dinner preparations were close to completion. The glorious scent of buttery garlic bread triggered a rumble from my stomach.

"Talk to you later. Dinner's almost ready."

"What are y'all having?"

"Homemade lasagna, salad, and garlic bread."

"I could be there in twenty minutes," he said.

"We're quarantined. Remember?"

After ending the call, I walked into the living room and straight into an onslaught of magnificent scents.

"Dinner's ready," Gina yelled.

I smiled when I saw the dining table set with fine china and flickering candles.

Latishia clapped and did a happy dance when she saw my expression. "Gina and I thought, why not celebrate such a wonderful meal. We even broke out your cloth napkins."

My smile widened. "That's great."

Gina carried in the baking dish of lasagna and set it on a trivet on the buffet server. The garlic bread was in a covered basket on the table, ready to be passed. Individual salads were in place.

Gina returned with a pinot grigio and started pouring some into the wine glasses. "Mom sent a couple of bottles of this because she knows it goes great with her pasta dishes."

We grabbed our plates and dished steaming, ooey-gooey lasagna onto them. The tangy scent of tomato sauce, coupled with the comforting smell of cheese, lifted my spirits like a warm hug. We took our places and blessed the food.

Latishia flipped back the cloth, uncovering the warm garlic bread. The savory aroma nearly sent me into a nasal orgasm.

"This is one good thing that comes from being quarantined with my best friends, whose parents are spectacular cooks." I raised my glass. "To Mama Bongiorno."

"Amen to that!" Latishia said, before taking a sip. "Good wine. This and the tasty food should help calm my pandemic anxiety."

Pandemic anxiety. I wonder if that diagnosis will make the next DSM Diagnostic Manual?

Kat poured Italian dressing over her salad. "Poor Jack. The schools are closed, and my parents are keeping a tight rein. He's doing his schoolwork online."

"Dante's complaining, too. He wants to play basketball in the park, but Mom and Dad won't let him because of social distancing. Aaron's working from home. He said he enjoys the commute down the hallway."

We chuckled.

"Is he even getting out of his pajamas?" I asked.

"Who knows?" Latishia reached for another slice of bread. "He's saving money on gasoline."

Gina sliced off a square of lasagna. "I talked to Anthony today. Mom's so worried that all she does is pray the rosary, cook, and clean. It's a good thing Pop bought her a larger freezer last Christmas."

Kat giggled. "Your mom can stock my freezer with her goodies anytime she wants. I can't believe my parents have taken such a liking to Italian food."

Gina laughed. "Our moms are trading recipes." She pointed her fork at me. "What did Mike say?"

"He thought it was funny that we have a toilet paper crisis."

They stopped eating and looked at me.

Latishia harrumphed. "He's such a man. Just because he can shake his wiener and go on, doesn't mean we can."

After the meal, Gina rubbed her stomach. "Tiramisu and coffee would be the perfect ending to this meal if I had a place to put it."

Kat pushed away from the table. "I can't eat another bite."

We gathered the dishes and took them to the kitchen. While Kat and I stored leftovers and washed the china, the latest news blared on the television.

I tossed the dishtowel into the washer and stretched. I was on my way to the living room when the doorbell rang. Buffy sprang to her feet and barked while racing to the door.

I turned on the porch light and peeked out. "It's Mike."

He backed away when I opened the door a smidgen. "Sorry I upset you." He pointed at a large gift-wrapped box on the walk. "Maybe this will get me out of the doghouse." He threw me a kiss, walked to his car, and drove away.

I yelled, "You can stop peeking out the curtains. He's gone."

I stepped outside, picked up the box, and carried it to the dining room where I placed it on the table. "It's not heavy."

Gina's eyes flashed with excitement. "I wonder what's inside."

"What did he say?" Latishia asked, rushing to join us.

"He apologized for upsetting me and hoped the present would get him out of the doghouse."

I pulled off the large bow. Due to the quality of the wrapping, I felt sure Rachael did it. I began loosening a corner of the paper.

"You drive me crazy!" Gina said. She grabbed the corner and ripped the paper.

I nudged her away. "It's my present!"

"Could be a bomb," Kat said, a twinkle in her eyes.

I finished removing the wrapping to reveal a plain cardboard box sealed with packing tape.

"Gina, get me a knife from the block on the counter."

She came back wielding the largest, longest one.

Latishia put a chair between them. "Sweet Baby Jesus! Are you planning a massacre?"

"Give me that. Talk about overkill." I took the knife and slit the tape, opened the flaps, and peeked inside.

Gina shoved curls out of her face. "What is it, for chrissake."

I pulled out a six-pack of toilet paper and held it aloft.

We whooped with excitement.

I texted Mike, *All is forgiven. Thanks*

CHAPTER 26: Day Two of Quarantine

The next morning, the clanging of Buffy's tags woke me. I peeked with one eye at the bedside clock. Six-thirty. Yawning, I sat up and petted Buffy. "My little fuzzy alarm clock."

Gina moaned and rolled over.

I decided to put on jeans and a shirt before making my way to the kitchen. To my surprise, Kat was dressed and filling her mug from the electric kettle.

She dunked her tea bag into the steaming water, releasing the fragrance of blood orange. "I would've started the coffee, but I don't know how."

"No problem. That tea smells wonderful."

"Tastes good, too."

Within minutes, the invigorating aroma of coffee filled the kitchen, infusing me with fond memories of Mom and Dad sitting at the breakfast table. As a child, I'd beg to try their coffee until Mom would relent and put one teaspoon of the brew into my milk.

Kat tucked her hair behind her ears. "Looks like we're getting the morning shift since we're the early risers. Big breakfast this morning?"

"Sure. Bacon and waffles?"

Kat squeezed the tea from the bag with a spoon and then set it on a small saucer for a second cup. "What goodies do you have to put into the waffles?"

I patted a yawn from my mouth. "Blueberries, pecans, and chocolate chips. What do you want in them?"

"Everything!"

I whirled to find Gina leaning against the doorframe.

Grinning, I said, "Sounds good to me."

By the time Latishia joined us, the table was set, the bacon was cooked, and the waffles were on the way to the table.

Latishia rubbed her eyes. "I could smell the bacon all the way back to the bedroom. I'm starving."

Gina winked at me. "You're always starving."

Latishia flipped her braids over a shoulder. "Genius requires fuel."

Waffles with blueberries, pecans, and chocolate are a tasty treat. The warm, comforting scent of vanilla, combined with the blueberries' tangy smell, triggered my mouth to water. Closing my eyes, I crunched into the pecans and let the semisweet chips melt on my tongue. I opened my eyes and smiled while chewing.

Kat wiped her mouth with a napkin. "The waffles are delicious. What's on the agenda today?"

Latishia reached for her mug. "My vacation ended last night. The bank is dropping my computer by this morning, so I can work from home. I need to check on some of my building loans. A lot can go wrong in eight days."

"That's a great idea, Latishia," Gina said. "I'll get my secretary to drop off my laptop, so I can work on some briefs and motions that need to be filed."

Latishia tipped her chin up. "Like I said, genius requires fuel."

"Those laptops need to be sanitized before they come in the house," Kat said, reaching for the syrup.

Gina sat straight and saluted. "Yes, ma'am."

I picked up my mug and headed toward the pot. "It's getting deep in here, and I don't mean philosophy."

When I returned, we cleared the table, so Gina and Latishia could clean up the mess. Kat and I took our drinks to the living room to watch the morning news. It was anything but relaxing.

My jaw dropped when the reporter showed a chart indicating the current confirmed COVID-19 cases in the nation. It seemed to have doubled overnight. "I can't believe how fast this virus is spreading."

Kat shook her head. "I'm astounded by the nationwide death rate. Glad I don't live or work as a nurse in New York." She sat back. "Dr. Howard is anxious for me to return to work. His practice could become quite busy between this virus and the flu." The mug of tea in her hand trembled. "I'm so glad I'm not working in the emergency room. What a zoo that could become."

"Sounds dangerous to me. It's like being on the front lines of battle in a war with an invisible enemy."

Kat pushed her glasses back in place. "It is dangerous. The only things between medical personnel and this virus are sanitation and PPE."

"What's PPE?" I asked.

"Medical talk for personal protective equipment. Remember all the stuff Doc was wearing when he gave us the tests?"

I remoted the television off. "This is too depressing. I hope my clients aren't fixated on these reports. It's enough to induce a panic attack."

Kat sighed and stood. "Since we have no work to do from home, want to do a puzzle?"

"Sure."

The only excitement during the day came from the deliveries of Latishia's and Gina's laptops. We all settled down to our separate activities. Mine included a nap.

Around five, we gathered in the living room while Gina set up a happy hour. She placed a divided plate with slices of carrots, celery, and bell pepper on the coffee table next to a bowl filled with ranch dressing.

"Yum," Kat said.

Gina did a little bow. "I know you love veggies."

Gina walked to the kitchen. We heard a pop. Minutes later, she returned, carrying a tray with four wine glasses and a bottle of zinfandel.

We loaded small paper plates with goodies and sipped wine.

"This is relaxing. One of my client's building loans for an apartment complex went south. More may be in trouble with the market taking a dive." Latishia tasted the wine. "Do y'all want to watch the news?"

"No!" the rest of us answered.

Gina gesticulated with a carrot stick. "I had difficulty sleeping last night after watching the news. I'm better equipped to handle bad news in the morning. Otherwise, I ruminate like a cow all night."

"Is that why you tossed and turned so much?" I asked.

Gina nodded and munched on a carrot.

"The whole pandemic makes me nervous. When I return to work, I don't want to pass the virus to Jack or my parents," Kat said.

The doorbell rang, sending Buffy into a frenzy.

Latishia's face brightened. "I bet that's Mom and Dad."

Mama Snide met Willy at his repair shop after Latishia's biological father was shot during a drug deal. They married, and Willy adopted Latishia. She's been his little princess ever since. The couple considers the rest of us to be their late-in-life daughters.

When we opened the door, Mama Snide, Willy, Dante, and Aaron stood by Mama Snide's catering van and waved. Several platters covered with aluminum foil and a large round container sat on the sidewalk.

Kat had to grab the back of Latishia's shirt to keep her from running to greet them.

To tell the truth, I could've used a Mama Snide hug. When she wraps you in her arms and sways from left to right, the world's troubles seem to melt away.

Willy yelled, "I hope y'all are in the mood for barbecue ribs."

Gina threw her arms in the air, looked toward heaven, and bellowed, "Yes! My prayers were answered."

Willy's wide grin said it all.

I whooped and did a little victory dance. Nobody makes ribs like Willy Snide, and no one enjoys eating them more than me.

Mama Snide laughed. "I thought a little soul food might cheer y'all up. There's also some macaroni and cheese and collard greens."

"Woohoo!" Kat said.

Dante yelled, "I love you, Mom," then looked around to see if anyone heard him.

"I love you, too, Sweetie. You behave for your grandparents."

Aaron and Latishia locked gazes. Electricity seemed to crackle between the two of them.

Gina poked Latishia in the side with a finger and whispered, "Cut that out, I'm about to have a vicarious orgasm watching y'all."

At six-foot-five, Aaron towered over the others like a mountain of ebony granite. "I miss you, Pumpkin. You'll be home soon."

Latishia threw him a kiss. "I miss my Honey Bear every day."

Unlike Dante, Aaron didn't seem a bit embarrassed.

Dante rolled his eyes and looked disgusted.

We yelled thank you and waved while they squeezed back into the van.

I thought, *There's nothing like having several sets of emotionally adopted parents who can cook.*

It wasn't until we hauled everything inside that I realized the Snides had included a chocolate cake.

Tears welled in Latishia's eyes when she saw it. "It's my favorite."

Since it was a forty-minute ride to my home from the Snides', we put the food into the microwave to warm. Twenty minutes later, we were seated with glasses of iced tea. We passed the food and loaded our plates. The aroma of the mac and cheese settled my nerves, but my main focus was the ribs. When the plate arrived, the tangy smell of Willy's sauce nearly made me swoon with delight. I grabbed four luscious ribs before passing them to Kat. I dished collards onto my plate and doused them with spicy pepper sauce. Salivating, I grabbed my fork and dug in.

There was little conversation, except for sounds of appreciation. We ran through several paper towels each, between licking sauce off our fingers.

When everyone had cleared their plates, I pushed away from the table and rubbed my distended stomach. "I don't know about y'all, I need to wait a bit for cake."

The Divas agreed.

After cleanup, we plodded to the living room to watch an action-adventure film. Midway, we paused the Harrison Ford flick to have cake. The heady aroma of chocolate brought a smile to my face. The moist cake and homemade icing sent my mood soaring. I thought, *Finally, a day without too much angst.*

My phone rang.

CHAPTER 27: Mike

My friends stopped eating cake and stared at my phone.

"It's Mike. Excuse me." I walked into the bedroom, closed the door, and answered. I hoped it was some good news.

"Hello, my Darling Fish Lips."

I rolled my eyes

"Have you heard anything about the test?" Mike asked, his tone hopeful.

"Not yet. Maybe tomorrow." I lay back on the bed to admire the sky and clouds I'd painted on the inside of my trey ceiling.

"I was thinking…"

"What?"

"When you're medically cleared, perhaps you could move in with me, since my house has more bedrooms. I want you to see what our life could be together." He lowered his voice. "I've heard rumors the governor will put a stay-at-home order into effect in a few days."

I propped up on one elbow. "Where did you hear that?"

He cleared his throat. "I can't reveal my source, but he's reliable."

Probably Madison's mayor. They play golf together. "Did your source say for how long?"

"Maybe a month. You see why it's important to move you in as soon as you're out of quarantine."

"You don't have a fenced yard for Buffy," I said. "Maybe you can stay here until this is over."

Silence.

"I was hoping your neighbor would watch the dog," he said.

I sat up and swung my legs over the bed. "My neighbor has already watched Buffy for a week. I don't want to impose. Besides, I miss her when she's not with me."

Using his 'be reasonable' tone, he said, "Phoenix, it's only a month or so."

The phrase, or so, didn't escape my attention. "So, Buffy's not welcome at your house? Is that what you're implying?" My chest felt tight.

Mike hemmed and hawed a bit. "The dog is nice and all. If you insist, we could get it a doghouse and kennel and put it in the backyard." He paused. "Dammit, it's a dog. I think it'd be happier outside. You could go out and visit it anytime you want."

It? When did my fluffy girl become an it? I'll admit, I didn't attempt to mitigate my displeasure. "Buffy loves *my house* with her dog door and fenced back yard. She wouldn't be happy cooped in a kennel, out in the elements."

He cleared his throat. "Be reasonable, Phoenix. Rachael's allergic to pet dander."

The 'be reasonable' comment irked me. I could feel anger fueling the hot flash building in my core like a steam-driven locomotive.

"I'm sorry to hear Rachael has allergies, but she has her own home. Mike, you need to understand something. Buffy is to me, what Rachael is to you. She's my four-legged, fluffy kid. She's family." My face burned as perspiration broke out on my forehead and upper lip. "Unlike Rachael, who is a grown woman with her own life, Buffy depends on me." I pulled my light sweater up to expose my midriff to the air. "Would you put your daughter outside in all kinds of weather?"

Silence.

I assumed Mike was red-faced and fuming at this point, since his M.O. is to clam up when he's trying to regain his composure. Usually, I sit out a silence, but I wanted some answers. "From your conversation, I can assume Rachael and the baby are still at your house?"

He lowered his voice. "Things aren't going well between her and Mark."

I ran my hand through my hair and turned on the ceiling fan before I plopped back and pulled a pillow under my head. *Not good.*

"What's going on with those two?" One bad habit of being a psychologist is I ask personal questions and expect answers.

The baby started wailing. Mike sighed. "Let me go to my room."

I put away some folded clothes while I waited.

"I can talk now. Mark is having an affair with another attorney at his law firm."

I sucked in a breath. I knew how it felt to have an unfaithful husband. "Is it over?"

"She hoped it was, but two days ago she found sexual texts and plans for the two to meet on his phone."

"The guy's an attorney, and he doesn't know any better than to use his phone for an affair?" I asked.

"She snooped around and found a second phone in the glove box of his car."

"Not good, sounds more like a love affair than a fling," I said, adjusting the pillow under my head.

"Seems like it. I can't believe Mark's willing to sacrifice his family for an easy…"

Silence.

"I know the F word, Mike. That's a shame. What's Rachael going to do?"

"She's wavering right now. We've hired an investigator to get the goods on Mark and this…this…"

"Slut?"

"That'll work. Phoenix, she's so depressed. She disappears into her room several times a day. I hear her crying in there. Is that normal?"

"For what's happening in her life, I'd say, yes. Did she have any post-partum depression before this started?" I asked.

"She was cheerful as a lark."

I thought, *That uncomplicates matters.* "Then it's probably normal relationship grief. I'd still keep an eye on her. People do crazy stuff during divorces."

"I'm afraid she might hurt herself," Mike said, his voice cracking.

"Has she made threats?" I asked, alarm tingling my senses.

"Not that I've heard."

"She loves her child, which would be a reason to live, with or without Mark. If she threatens suicide, I'd see it as a possible manipulative tactic to guilt Mark back into the relationship. Not that it shouldn't be taken seriously. People accidentally die from attention-seeking suicide attempts all the time. Did she follow through on my suggestion to see a therapist to help cope with this?"

"I'm not sure. I'll ask. I'd feel better if you were here," he said. "You could talk to her and monitor the situation."

I wondered, *Does he want me, or a built-in therapist for his daughter?*

"How long will she be staying with you?" I asked, fearful of the answer.

With a gruff tone, he said, "Until the outcome is decided. I told Rachael if they divorce, there's no reason to move. She could live with us, and we would help raise the baby."

Nice of him to volunteer me without discussing it first. He wants an in-house therapist, babysitter, and lady friend. "Mike, I think we both need to think about what we want long-term and what we're willing to tolerate."

He huffed. "It's all about the damn dog, isn't it?"

A chill drizzled down my back. Mike's words were cold.

I can't believe he's acting this way.

"Phoenix, it's just a mutt. Can't you give it to one of your friends?"

Mutt! When did my Cocker Spaniel become a mutt? Through clenched teeth, I said, "No. Mike, this is about much more than Buffy. I need to go."

"Oh, come on, Phoenix!"

I disconnected, slid to the carpet, and pulled Buffy close. Burying my face in her fur, I cried. Her warmth and doggie scent offered needed solace. This little dog had comforted me through my Dad's death, my divorce from Todd, my recent breakup from Brent, and now, this revealing conversation with Mike. *This is a new side of him and I don't like it. Not one little bit.*

Gina knocked and popped her head around the door. "Is everything okay in here?"

I looked up, tears cascading down my cheeks, and shook my head.

"Merda!" She threw the door open and knelt next to me. "What happened?"

Latishia appeared in the doorway. "Don't start to explain until we all get there."

She and Kat came in and sat on the floor, circling me. I gave them the brief version.

Latishia's brows formed a V. "He doesn't understand, 'love me, love my dog?' What's wrong with that man?" She crossed her arms. "Is this the new pandemic side of Mike?"

"Maybe," I said, wiping tears from my eyes with my sleeve.

Gina rubbed circles on my back. "So, you're expected to move to his house, give up yours, give Buffy away, and live happily ever after being Rachael's therapist and babysitter?"

"Sounds like it." I dabbed under my eyes with the tissue.

Kat handed me the box. "That's a crappy deal."

Gina winked. "You know if you give me Buffy, you can visit anytime you want."

I squeezed Buffy tight against me and gave her a squinty-eyed glare. "No way."

"When are you going to talk to him again?" Kat shrugged. "There may be extenuating circumstances."

The phone's ringtone announced a call from Mike.

"Not tonight, that's for sure. Nobody puts my Buffy in peril."

CHAPTER 28: Day Three

The next morning, I woke feeling bloopy and congested from crying. I dragged myself out of bed and wandered through the living room toward the kitchen, with Buffy prancing beside me.

Kat sat at the small table in my breakfast nook with a mug of tea, frowning at her phone. She looked up. "How many times did Mike call last night?"

I yawned. "Six or seven that I know about. The do not disturb mode went on at ten-thirty." I reached down to put food in Buffy's bowl.

She doggie smiled before gulping it down.

"Do you think he realized his mistake and has changed his mind?" Kat raised her glasses and rubbed her left eye.

I shrugged. "Mike was so different. Even his tone of voice. He's always been focused on getting what he wants. I used to think it was me because he loved me. Last night, I felt it was about Rachael and how I fit into his plans to save his daughter."

"Somehow, I always thought you two would marry. There's a certain chemistry between y'all." Kat stood and looked around the kitchen. "What do you want to fix for breakfast?"

"I'm in the mood for some hot, comforting oatmeal."

Thirty minutes later, Gina and Latishia walked into the kitchen.

Gina brushed curls off her forehead and said, "Coffee," in a hoarse voice.

Latishia followed behind her. "Me, too. What's for breakfast?" She raised her nose and sniffed. "I don't smell any bacon."

I raised the spoon in my hand. "That's because we have oatmeal."

Latishia scrunched her nose. "Oatmeal? Can't we have something good?"

I shooed her out of the kitchen. "We'll bring it to the table."

I ladled a generous amount into each bowl, giving Latishia a bit more than the rest.

Kat carried each steaming bowl to the dining table using oven mitts. After I ran water into the pot to keep the oatmeal remnants from hardening into concrete, I took a fresh mug of coffee to the table and sat.

Latishia squinted at her oatmeal, stabbing it again and again with her spoon.

I chuckled. "It's already dead, Latishia. No need to kill it with a blunt instrument."

Gina stirred it around, sending spirals of steam toward the ceiling. She leaned closer, sniffed, and smiled. "I smell apples, cinnamon, and nutmeg."

Kat chewed, her head cocked to the side. "It's like apple crumble with pecans."

Latishia's head jerked up. "Did you say, apple crumble?" She took a small amount onto her spoon and tasted it. "It looks like oatmeal, only it tastes good."

We focused on eating, which meant I didn't have to field questions about Mike.

I was on my second cup of coffee when Latishia announced, "That was the best oatmeal I've ever eaten. Don't tell Mama, but it beat hers hands down."

I tilted my head. "That's quite a compliment, since she's such a fantastic cook."

Gina licked the last oatmeal off her spoon. "I agree with Latishia. Mom is an excellent cook, but she does despicable things to oatmeal. Hers looks and tastes like wallpaper paste."

Latishia chuckled. "How do you know what wallpaper paste tastes like?"

"I ate some when I was little."

Kat screwed up her face. "Yuck!"

I said, "Words of wisdom to the cleanup crew. Put water to the top of each bowl and submerge the spoons for ten minutes or so to make washing them easier."

Kat and I wandered into the living room with our hot drinks and turned on the news. The nationwide confirmed cases of the virus were still rising, along with the death rate. Italy remained on lockdown, yet people were still dying. Spain was also in dire trouble.

My hand covered my heart. "I don't understand. If Italy is quarantined, why are the numbers of cases and deaths still rising?"

A commercial came on, so Kat muted the TV. "From what I've been able to research, there can be a two-week delay from infection to symptoms. Most hospital stays are eight to ten days, longer than inpatient stays for this year's seasonal flu. Therefore, the figures will lag for two or more weeks. The isolation has to be helping to control the spread, only we can't see the evidence yet."

She turned the volume back on. The confirmed cases and deaths were escalating in the United States, especially in New York, Illinois, Washington, Florida, and Louisiana.

I looked at her. "Louisiana?"

She pointed at the screen. "Listen."

Despite the threat of the new coronavirus, New Orleans leaders had gone ahead with Mardi Gras. Thousands of drunk people had crowded together on the streets and in bars and restaurants. The spike in cases two weeks later was the direct result of that decision.

I threw my hands in the air. "What were they thinking?"

"What were who thinking?" Gina asked. She walked past me to occupy her usual seat. She snuggled down with a mug of java.

The scent drifted my way, making me consider another cup. "New Orleans had Mardi Gras in the middle of a pandemic," I said.

Latishia sank onto the love seat. "I can answer that question." She rubbed the fingertips of her right hand together. "Money. It's the year's largest money-maker for them."

I shook my head. "I hope it was worth the loss of life."

Kat muted the TV again. "Hindsight is twenty-twenty. Humans have a wonderful capacity for denial when it comes to fun."

"I agree with Kat." Gina pointed at the TV. "The announcer said one of the reasons for the high numbers in Florida was the influx of college students to the state for spring break."

I ran my hands through my hair. "Good grief! Why aren't parents stopping them?"

"My Jack wouldn't have been there." Kat pushed her glasses back in place. She jutted her jaw forward. "I wouldn't have allowed it."

Latishia crossed her arms. "Same here."

"There's a pattern here, beyond sheer stupidity and greed," I said.

Gina leaned closer. "What?"

"Each of these states has international airports or cruise ship ports."

"That's true," said Gina. "If that's the case, there should be spikes in North Carolina and Texas, because they have international airports."

A news story caught our attention. People were dying without loved ones, and mourners wouldn't be allowed a standard funeral due to social distancing.

I swiped a tear from my eye. "I hope this mess improves soon. This is heartbreaking."

Twenty minutes later, the doorbell rang. Buffy skidded out of the kitchen before gaining some purchase on the living room carpet. She growled with enthusiasm when she hit the hardwood in the foyer. Losing traction, she slid butt first into the door and yelped.

We laughed. I walked over and checked on her. "Poor baby."

"Phoenix! I need to talk to you," Mike yelled.

CHAPTER 29: The Take Over

We froze and exchanged worried looks. Latishia stood and began easing toward her room, I suspected to have the best view of the upcoming encounter with Mike.

I picked up Buffy and handed her to Gina. After a quick peek through the peephole, I yelled, "Mike, back up, and I'll come out."

He retreated, holding up his hands in a gesture of surrender.

I opened the door and took two steps out to the porch.

He rushed in, picked me up, and carried me into the foyer.

I froze while trying to catch my breath and find my voice.

After he placed me back on my feet, he shut the door with his foot, and grinned, exposing his dimples to full magnitude.

My temples pounded to the marching beat of my heart. "What in the world are you—"

He pressed a finger to my lips.

I batted away his hand.

He wrapped me in a hug. "I had to see you," he whispered in my ear.

His arms felt terrific around me. Comforting, after hearing all the horrific news about the virus. Taking a deep breath, I exhaled and pushed him back. "You fool! You may have infected yourself with the virus."

His jaw flexed. "I don't give a damn. We need to talk." He crossed his arms. "So, I'm exposed. No biggie. If you're cleared today, that means I'm free of the virus, too. If not, I'll be quarantined here with you."

I glanced over at the Divas. Gina held a squirming Buffy with the thin-lipped expression that often preceded a temper outburst, complete with colorful Italian expletives.

Kat's brows were drawn together.

Latishia had crossed her arms over her chest. She took a step forward, looking capable of delivering a nasty Diva slap.

Kat stepped in front and held her arms out to keep them away from us. "Stay back."

Latishia's lip protruded. "Why? He's already had contact with Phoenix."

Kat held her ground. "We may be negative. We don't know who or what he's been exposed to at this point." She turned to Mike. "Have you been tested?"

He shot her a defiant look before shaking his head.

"Have you been sick, run a fever, or had a cough?" Kat asked, lowering her arms.

"Only sinus symptoms. I'm sure it's allergies. Besides, if I get the coronavirus, it's just the flu. No biggie."

Kat tucked one side of her hair behind an ear and frowned. "Have you been self-isolating?"

Mike had his arm around my waist, unwilling to let go. I looked at him. His jaw muscle jumped. "Sorta."

Gina's hands fisted on her hips. "What does, sorta, mean?"

Mike cleared his throat. "Well, I've been to the Mayor's office a couple of times, gone to the grocery almost every day, made a couple of trips to Lowe's this week, and had coffee at the Sunnyside a few mornings with the guys."

Gina huffed and gave him one of her famous eye rolls. "Merda!"

Kat raised her phone. "I'm phoning Dr. Howard to see if our test results came in yet." She jerked her head toward Mike. "I'll also see if I can get 'Mr. Sorta Isolated' tested."

"I'm not sick!" He turned his head and coughed, before tightening his hold on me.

My friends backed further away. Latishia disappeared and returned, spraying Lysol into the space between us.

Kat sighed. "Mike, haven't you been watching the news? Some people are asymptomatic carriers."

His eyes widened. He released me.

I stepped six feet away from him. *Probably too late now.*

Kat spoke in low tones to Dr. Howard. I couldn't overhear the conversation, but her nods and frowns weren't reassuring.

She disconnected the call. "Doc said he expects our results to come in this afternoon." She pointed the phone toward Mike. "Dr. Howard isn't happy about your foolhardy move. He wants you at his office ASAP. He has some kits available and is willing to test you. You're to return home and isolate yourself from anyone in your household."

"Can't I stay here?" he asked, looking from her to me.

Kat ignored the question. "Phoenix, I'm sorry, but we have to isolate you to your room until we leave." She turned to Gina. "This means you need to move all your things out, pronto."

Gina glared at Mike. "Stupido, idiota!" She whirled and stomped toward the bedroom to pack.

Latishia grinned. "I don't need any help translating that one."

Mike raised his chin and crossed his arms. "I still don't see why this is a big deal."

Kat ignored his comment. "Thanks to Mike's rash actions, you're quarantined an additional three days or more until his test results come in."

Anger rampaged through my system like a fiery lava flow destined to ignite the whole house. Thank goodness it was a hot flash and not real lava. I used one sleeve to dab my forehead before pushing them up to bare my overheated arms. *I agree with Gina, he's a stupido idiota.*

Sounds of slamming drawers and Italian cursing came from my bedroom. Latishia stink-eyed Mike, Lysol can at the ready. He'd be lucky to escape without being fumigated. While Kat looked calm and contained, her tapping foot betrayed her underlying anger.

"Let me get this straight," I said. "Even if my test comes back negative, I'm quarantined until *his* test comes back negative?"

Kat nodded. "You work with patients in a small room for up to an hour. If you're positive, you run the risk of infecting eight or more people a day. Then you'd have to add the number of people each of them can infect in two weeks. Better safe than sorry."

I ran my hands through my hair. "You're right. I have to consider the safety of my staff and patients."

Kat lasered a glare at Mike that should've incinerated him on the spot. "Phoenix, pray it comes back negative, or you'll have to isolate for an additional two weeks and lose that much more income." She held up her phone. "Mike, give me your mobile number."

He rattled it off to her.

"I'm texting Dr. Howard's phone number and address to you. Phone him when you arrive. He'll send someone to your car with the proper forms to fill out. The nurse will perform the test there to protect the staff and other patients. I've asked him to provide a release of information, so he can inform Phoenix about the outcome of your test. Please sign it."

Still fuming, I mumbled, "Three more days of isolation. This means I have to cancel three more days of appointments. What if those people really need me?"

Latishia shook the Lysol can. "If this idiot keeps screwing up, you may go broke."

Mike gave Latishia the cold shoulder and faced Kat. His jaw muscles flexed. "I don't understand why I can't isolate here with Phoenix. If y'all are cleared later today, there will be plenty of room. It'll also be safer for Rachael and the baby."

Kat eyed him with cold deliberation, then looked at me. "It's your decision. His daughter needs to be tested anyway. He should have been more careful with an infant in the house."

CHAPTER 30: Delicious Aromas

I crossed my arms and glowered at Mike. "I'm really pissed right now. I suggest you leave this minute and head to Dr. Howard's office."

He stepped forward and rubbed his hand down my arm, causing my whole body to tingle. I thought, *It's been too long, girl. Maybe I should let him stay if we test negative.*

"My Darling Fish Lips, I couldn't stand the separation. I've missed you."

My inner psychologist kicked in. *Letting him stay will only reinforce his bad behavior.*

I shrugged off his hand and backed away. "Go now. I'm too angry to talk."

His shoulders drooped. He looked down and shook his head. "I've made things worse for you." Looking me in the eyes, he said, "Sorry." He turned and walked out the door.

Latishia rushed forward, spraying a liberal amount of Lysol into the air. I backpedaled and waved the cloud of disinfectant away from me.

Buffy yelped once, before high-tailing it toward the kitchen, sneezing the whole way.

Kat wiped down everything Mike had touched before locking the door.

Several hours later, I was sulking in my room when the doorbell rang again.

I yelled loud enough to be heard through my closed door, "If that's Mike, tell him to go away. I'm still mad at him."

My friends sounded excited.

"Wonder what's going on? Geez, I'm already talking to myself."

Sometime later, Gina tapped on the door and yelled, "Your lunch is outside the door. Kat's family delivered it."

"So that is what all the excitement was about." I opened the door and found a TV tray with a plate full of steaming food, iced tea, and everything needed to enjoy my meal. I placed the laden tray on a table I'd set up in front of a chair, with a view of the television. I nearly swooned as the spicy scents surrounded me. Any minute I would start drooling. Chicken fried rice, General Tso's chicken, beef and broccoli, and sautéed veggies were mounded onto my plate. Tears of gratitude welled in my eyes. Kat's family had cooked each of our favorite dishes. Mine was the chicken fried rice.

I flipped to Prime Video. I didn't want to ruin an excellent meal with coronavirus reports. I picked *Burn Notice* and sat back to watch Michael Westen's adventures while trying to discover who caused him to lose his job with the CIA. I sighed, feeling a tad down. The Divas were enjoying the meal together, while I was stuck alone in this bedroom. I jabbed a fork into the beef. "Thanks a lot, Mike."

The moment the beef entered my mouth, I closed my eyes to better appreciate the flavor and banned him from my thoughts. "Nothing is going to spoil this."

By the end of the show, I'd finished the meal. I felt sated, and a sense of wellbeing enveloped me. I turned off the television, placed the tray outside my door, and snuggled under the covers for a nap.

***

Rapping on the door woke me from a dream. I sat up feeling drowsy. "What?"

"Dr. Howard called." Kat's voice sounded upbeat. "We're all negative."

I jumped out of bed and did a victory dance. Standing close to the door, I said, "That's great! I'm so relieved we didn't spread anything through all those airports."

"Me, too," Kat said. "I texted Peru Tourism with the good news. We've packed up to go home. I can't wait to see Jack and my parents. I start back to work tomorrow."

"Tell Dr. Howard, thanks for everything. Please be careful and wear protective equipment," I said.

"I will. Can't be too careful."

"We really appreciate you letting us isolate here," Gina said. "We're leaving you all the leftovers, so you should be able to eat for at least a week without cooking."

Tears welled in my eyes. I'd miss my friends. "Thanks. At least I have something to look forward to."

Latishia said, "If you need anything, you let us know. We'll be using FaceTime to stay in touch. I can't wait to see everyone. It's going to be a hot time tonight!"

I laughed, imagining Latishia doing a bootie dance. "Be safe. Bye."

"We'll lock the door on the way out." Kat chuckled. "Try not to go stir crazy."

A few minutes later, I heard the front door close. When I left the confinement of the bedroom, Buffy pranced around my feet. I reached down and picked her up. "It's just us, Girl."

CHAPTER 31: *What to Do?*

I was in the middle of a movie when Mike's unique ring played on my phone. I frowned at it. His foolhardy act still upset me. Because of him, I'd had to cancel at least three more days of patient appointments. When I phoned the answering service to give them the bad news, I learned that a third of my patients had already canceled because of coronavirus concerns.

The phone stopped ringing.

I settled deeper into my chair and focused on a fast-paced action scene.

It rang again.

Huffing my frustration, I paused the movie and answered. "I had to cancel three days of patient appointments because of you! Are you happy?"

An interminable pause.

"No," Mike said, sounding contrite. "Was your test negative?"

"Yes, but I'm still in quarantine because of *you*." I gritted my teeth to keep from yelling.

"My Darling Fish Lips, I can help ease your pain."

To my surprise, my body revved with anticipation. *Stop it*, I told myself. *This man has interfered with your patients, denied you a sizable amount of income, and limited your mobility.*

"Rachel wants me to leave to protect the baby," he said, sounding downcast.

I rolled my eyes. "In case you've forgotten, that's your home. She needs to go back to her house."

"She doesn't think she can. Mark is acting erratically."

I huffed. "More reason for you to stay at your place and defend your daughter."

"She's upset with me right now."

She's not the only one, I thought, but I didn't utter a word. Time stretched like a rubber band.

"Please!" Mike sounded frantic.

I took a deep breath and ran a hand through my hair. "What are your other options?"

"A motel." He didn't sound enthusiastic. "Pretty, please! I'll clean the house, wash the clothes—anything. Don't make me isolate alone in a tiny hotel room."

I sighed. The logical part of my brain waved red flags and yelled, *no!* My emotional side wanted to rescue Mike from his plight. Then there was the Neanderthal section that thought of passionate romps in bed. I shook my head to clear it. "Okay, but just until your test results come back."

"And if it's positive?"

I frowned. "I'd run for cover if I were you."

"Understood."

"When do you plan to arrive?" I asked, already regretting my decision.

The doorbell rang. I walked to the door to peep out. Mike stood on my porch, his dimples in full glory.

Irked, I yanked open the door.

He stood with a suitcase and a plastic grocery bag under his arm. He set the baggage down and whipped out a package of T.P. with a flourish. "I come in peace, bearing toilet paper." His sexy grin widened.

I blocked the entrance and plopped my hands on my hips. "I thought an olive branch was traditional."

"Not during a pandemic. Can I come inside?"

Still miffed, I grumbled under my breath and stepped aside.

He headed toward my bedroom.

"Hold up there." I ran in front of him and pointed at the guest bedroom.

He put his luggage on the carpet. "Give me a break, Phoenix."

I pointed the way.

He took a step toward me, arms open, eyes twinkling with mischief.

I held up my hand in a stop gesture. "The guest room, or you can leave. After what you did, toilet paper only gets you so far."

His shoulders slumped. Picking up the case, he walked inside and closed the door.

Buffy came through the dog door. When she made it to the living area, she smelled the air, scampered to the foyer, and sniffed Mike's path to the guest room. She sneezed twice, shaking her head, and looked at me.

I walked into my bedroom with Buffy on my heels. After slamming the door with the vengeance of any petulant adolescent, I locked it.

I snuggled into the pillows on my bed and called Kat. "I hate to bother you, but I've got a bit of a situation. Should I isolate from Mike?" I filled her in on what had happened.

I could imagine her shaking her head. "I knew he'd talk you into it. You're too kind-hearted. You've had close contact several times. There's no reason to stay apart."

"I thought a night of delayed gratification might teach him a lesson. I'm still upset."

"Call if you need me. It sounds like you have a plan." Kat laughed.

I said goodbye, burrowed deeper into the pillows, and napped.

CHAPTER 32: The Big Freeze

I woke, stretched, and thought about Mike bulldozing his way into my home this morning, and then wheedling his way in the second time this afternoon. I'd agreed to let him stay until the test results came in, but discovering he was standing on my porch while he played on my kindness rankled. He might be ex-military, but I knew a bit about strategy myself. I wanted him to take my concerns, issues, and Buffy into consideration.

I opened the door and followed Buffy to the kitchen. She stopped at her empty bowl and yipped. Her luminous brown eyes were wide with anticipation and need.

Who could resist, especially when it was her standard mealtime? I filled her food and water bowls.

While I was washing my hands like a surgeon, a noise caught my attention. I turned and found Mike standing at the entrance to the kitchen. His dark hair was tousled in a sexy, just out of bed way. Tight jeans topped by a tee-shirt made him tempting, like an hors d'oeuvre ready to be plucked from a platter. The song "Anticipation" played in my head.

"Is it all right for me to leave my room?" He smiled, those dimples working their magic.

"Only if you help with dinner."

His smile widened.

I pointed at the sink. "First, thoroughly wash your hands."

While he did, I pulled out lettuce, a tomato, and some celery. I'd placed the cutting board and a knife on the counter by the time he finished.

Handing him a towel, I said, "We will have separate hand towels. Yours will be the darker one."

"Roger that."

"If you'll make the salad, I'll take care of the rest. We're having leftover lasagna that Gina's mom made and garlic bread."

"Sounds delicious."

We worked in silence since I wasn't in a chatty mood. We had serious issues to discuss, and I wasn't sure I was ready. I set the table and filled the glasses with iced tea. Wine might give him the wrong idea, and I needed to keep my defenses up.

The entire room was infused with scents of garlic and tomato sauce, making it smell like an Italian restaurant.

I glanced over. "The salad looks good. The fresh veggies go back in the produce drawer."

"Can do." Mike toted them to the fridge.

I pulled the bubbling lasagna from the microwave and placed it on a trivet on the small breakfast table.

The oven timer binged. When I opened the door, heat and garlic butter blasted my face. I pulled it out, placed it on the stove, and fanned my face with the potholder. "Phew!"

Mike touched my arm, sending a zing along my nerve endings.

"Are you okay? You look flushed."

I shrugged his hand off my arm. "I'm fine." I placed the bread in a towel-lined basket and carried it to the table. Mike had already put the salads and Italian dressing on the table.

"Let's eat. You're in for a treat."

Mike took his seat. A moment later, he smiled and winked. "I'm hoping for dessert afterward."

I cocked my head and gave him my most seductive look. "Why, of course." *Don't get your hopes too high. I'm not on the menu.*

He straightened in his seat and reached across the table.

Instead of taking his hand, I picked up my fork. "There's ice cream in the freezer."

He made a grumbling noise and withdrew his hand. After his first bite of lasagna, his eyes went wide. "Mama Mia!"

"Too hot?"

He shook his head. "Gina's mom should open a restaurant. It's the best I've ever tasted."

"I'll let Gina know you approve." I poured dressing on my salad.

Mike reached for the garlic bread and crunched into a slice. "Mmm. You weren't kidding when you said I was in for a treat. I thought you ladies were suffering during your quarantine. Instead, y'all were eating like queens."

I gave him the stink-eye. "Of course, we suffered. The quarantine kept us from our families and our work, and reduced our income."

He looked down. "Sorry about my foolish behavior. I didn't think about the ramifications to you and Rachael, or I'd have been more careful. I've always been so healthy. I guess I was too cocky."

You're cocky, all right. "Mike, this is a pandemic. People are dying all over the world. The experts don't have enough information to tell us how to protect ourselves or how long this will last." I put down my fork. "We'd probably be infected from our exposure in Lima if it hadn't been for Kat. She made us avoid the sick tourist and had us sanitizing everything. We had a bit of luck, too. The Spanish-speaking tourists were separated from the English-speaking ones by the tour guides." An insight hit me. *I bet all the people in the sick guy's group were infected.*

He grinned. "For such a tiny woman, she's a force. She'd make a great general."

"All the Divas have special strengths," I said, still thinking about the rest of the folks on our Lima tour.

He ran a hand through his hair. "Look, I'm really sorry. I don't know how to make this up to you?"

Looking him in the eye, I said, "This recent stunt is only one issue we need to resolve. I need some space tonight. I'm willing to discuss this more tomorrow."

A sorrowful look filled his eyes. The "Buffy look" was amateur compared to his.

"Cheer up," I said. "There's chocolate ice cream for dessert."

"Maybe it'll cool down my passion," Mike mumbled, pouring dressing over his salad.

CHAPTER 33: Melting Ice

The next morning, I smiled when I opened my eyes to the painting on my ceiling. I hummed "Blue Skies" while dressing and applying makeup. *Only two more days of isolation.*

Buffy pranced and whined as she led the way to the kitchen. The sunlight streaming through the windows made stripes of light on the carpet, while dust fairies danced on the sunbeams.

Mike showed up after the coffee started brewing. He ran his hands through his hair, then stretched, causing his back to pop. "What are the breakfast options?"

I opened the fridge and looked around. "Ham and cheese omelet with toast?"

"Works for me."

"Good. You can set the table and make the toast. Don't forget to wash up. I may wash the skin off my hands before this virus goes away," I said.

He stifled a yawn before turning on the water to wash his hands.

Twenty minutes later, we were ready to eat.

Mike sat and sipped coffee while watching me doctor mine.

"Am I still in the doghouse?" he asked.

"I don't put dogs in a tiny abode to weather the elements." I forked a bite of omelet into my mouth, chewed, and swallowed. "In your case, I used the guest room."

We ate in silence. Famished, I dug in with gusto.

The feeder outside the window provided entertainment. Purple finches dropped in for a snack. Pecking daintily, they dropped seed down to the heavier doves that puttered around the ground cleaning up the mess. All was calm until a pair of cardinals swooped in, scaring the smaller birds away in a flutter of wings.

Before I realized it, my plate was empty. I rubbed my stomach. "That was yummy."

Mike set his fork on his cleared plate and sat back. "I agree."

We eyed each other while sipping coffee. I wasn't sure what issue to address first.

Mike unexpectedly broke the silence. "Can't we focus on our feelings for each other and not worry about the rest?"

My heart hammered in my chest. *What are my feelings for this man? There's sexual chemistry— always has been. Is that enough to make a life with another person?*

I put down my mug, remembering his temper tantrum at Jim and Nick's. "Feelings are only part of a successful relationship."

"How can your feelings be clear as long as you're seeing that other guy? What do I have to do? Why won't you let him go?"

How much do I reveal? Where to start? I blurted, "He's no longer in my life."

Mike's mouth dropped open, then lifted into a smile. "Since when?"

"Since Peru."

His brows knitted together. "You went to Peru with him?" The tone was part incredulous, part angry.

I shook my head. "I went to Peru with the Divas. We came back from Machu Picchu late one night and found him in the lobby of our hotel in Sacred Valley."

"What did he want?" Mike sat back in his chair and crossed his arms, preparing for the answer.

I sighed. "He received a promotion, which means he's moving to Seattle."

"Washington?"

"Yes. Brent proposed in the lobby and asked me to move there with him," I said in one breath.

Mike leaned forward, his gaze burning into mine. "What did you say?"

"Nothing at first, because I fainted."

Mike jerked upright. "Fainted! Were you sick?"

"It was a combination of high-altitude sickness, low blood sugar, dehydration, and shock."

Mike shifted in his seat, looking aggravated. "Dammit, woman, did you say yes or no?"

"No."

Melting back into his seat, Mike looked relieved. "So, he's out of the running?"

"I wasn't aware it was a competition?" I said.

"When it involves a desirable woman, it's war. I can't believe I let the guy get the drop on me. That was a brilliant move to show up in Peru and propose." He rubbed his chin. "Wish I'd thought of it."

I rolled my eyes. *Thank goodness you didn't. That's all I needed was two of you crashing a Diva vacation.*

Mike rose, leaned across the small table, and kissed me. His warm mouth tasted of coffee.

I stiffened but then fell into the kiss, losing all my inhibitions. When I opened my eyes, Mike was lifting me to carry me to the bedroom.

It'd been weeks since we were together. Excitement zinged through my body, flaming my passion. Mike's hair smelled of coconut shampoo, reminding me of our first date in Florida.

He placed me on the rumpled sheets and joined me.

"My Darling Fish Lips, prepare to be ravished."

CHAPTER 34: New Revelations

I lay on my back with my wrist resting on my forehead, trying to reconstruct how a discussion over coffee had ended in a frantic romp in bed. I ran my other hand over the smooth microfiber sheet while I thought. True, it had been several weeks without sexual contact, but this session of lovemaking seemed different somehow. The word "desperate" came to mind.

"That was great!" Mike rolled over and smiled at me, dimples doing their magic. "I've missed you. There was a hole in my life with you gone."

His last statement caused my stomach to rollercoaster, but not in a good way. Unaware of my unease, Mike prattled on.

"I'm relieved that Brent guy is out of the picture." He ran his finger down my face. "Now we can move forward with our plans."

Our plans? Don't you mean yours?

"I can't wait to tell Rachael. She really likes you." He rolled over and stood. I admired his broad shoulders and narrow waist as he disappeared into the bathroom.

He does stay in shape, I conceded. I didn't want another Todd, who kept expanding beyond his waistband and wedding ring.

Mike returned, comfortable with his nakedness.

Before he could reach for me, I scooted out of bed, headed toward the restroom, and closed the door behind me. I lowered to the toilet and discovered the seat wasn't there, plunging bootie first into icy water that smelled of urine. My screech should've alerted the entire subdivision to my plight.

Mike's feet pounded the floor. He threw open the door and stopped, mouth agape.

Embarrassed beyond words, I struggled to free myself from the frigid, stinking water.

He didn't help me. Instead, he stood there and stared. A chuckle rumbled in his chest and progressed to a gut-wrenching, tear-producing guffaw.

I wasn't amused. Fuming from anger and humiliation, I extracted myself from the toilet and slammed down the lid.

Noticing my fury, Mike kept saying "Sorry," between bouts of giggles.

Flames raced to my face. I pointed toward the door. "Out!"

After I flushed the toilet, the pain on my lower spine drew my attention. I rubbed the area and winced. I turned on the water in the shower and waited for it to warm. While I scrubbed, all I could think about was Mike's three inconsiderate actions. First, he didn't lower the seat. "We've discussed this, and he started lowering the seat. Why the hell didn't he do it this time?"

Second, he didn't flush the toilet. "Didn't his mother raise him right? He's a grown man, not a child for goodness' sake." Third, he laughed instead of helping me. "He just stood there and left me to struggle out of that toilet."

I toweled off and turned to inspect the developing bruise on my lower vertebrae in the mirror. After applying makeup and drying my hair, I walked into the bedroom to find my discarded clothes.

Mike sat on the bed looking somewhat contrite between eruptions of chuckles.

I plopped my fists on my naked hips and glared at him. "Excuse me if I fail to find falling into icy, piss-filled water amusing. We've had the toilet seat discussion before. And why didn't you flush, for chrissakes!"

He shrugged. "I never do if I don't use paper."

I ran both hands through my hair. "This is an issue for me."

He sighed and stood. "You're making a mountain out of a molehill. You landed in some cold water, no biggie. No harm was done."

I turned and pointed at my lower back. "This bruise doesn't count as harm done?"

It felt like he poked the spot.

"Ow!" I cringed from the stabbing pain and moved away.

"I'm sorry, I didn't realize you were hurt."

I whirled. "Oh, I nearly forgot. Thanks for helping me out of the toilet." Snatching my clothes from where they were flung, I stomped back into the bathroom and slammed the door. *Calm down. Stop acting like a raging adolescent.* I stayed in there twenty minutes while regaining my composure.

When I returned to the living room, Mike had claimed squatter's rights to my recliner.

I stood in front of him and crossed my arms. *After all that, you're sitting in my chair?*

He craned his neck to look around me.

I cleared my throat.

He focused on me with a quizzical expression.

"How many times have you visited my home?"

He frowned and looked up as if the magic number floated below the ceiling. "Quite a few."

"You should know by now, that's my chair." *Geez, even the Divas respect the sanctity of my recliner.*

He shrugged. "I sit in the recliner at my house. I didn't think you'd mind." His tone hinted that I was being unreasonable.

My back hurts. I need my recliner. "I, too, sit in the recliner at my house. So, if you get to claim my recliner when you visit here, does that mean I get to claim yours when I visit your home?"

His scowl showed what he thought of that idea. "Do you want me to move?"

"Yes, my back hurts." I rubbed the spot. "I want to use *my* recliner."

He huffed and dropped the footrest before heaving himself from the chair. Shuffling a few steps, he plopped on the couch and returned his attention to the show about the stock market.

I settled into the recliner and elevated my feet. I had to shift a bit to avoid pressure on my injury. After a quick glance at Mike, I texted Gina. *Mike is isolating at my house until his test comes back.*

Since we'd returned home from Peru, Gina had discovered face emojis. The text response showed an emoji with long, dark curly hair and big brown eyes wearing a shocked expression.

I blew up this morning. I briefly explained the toilet and chair incidents.

A face with a mushroom cloud exploding from the top of the head filled my screen. She texted, *Let's talk at ten.*

I sent a thumbs up.

CHAPTER 35: Rachael

At ten o'clock, my cell phone jingled Gina's ring tone. I dropped the footrest and grabbed the device. "Excuse me, I need to take this call."

Mike grunted, never taking his eyes from the television screen.

Buffy joined me in the bedroom before I closed and locked the door.

Gina sounded huffy. "Took you long enough to answer."

"I waited until I was in the bedroom. What's your take on Mike's behavior?"

I climbed on the bed, fluffed the pillows, and leaned against them before Buffy jumped up to cuddle against me. Birds chirped a merry song outside the window.

"Sounds different than his usual way of acting. Did he leave the toilet seat up before?" Gina asked.

I nodded as if she could see me. "Once, the first time he came to my house. I discussed it with him, and he never did it again, at least not when I was around." I stroked Buffy's smooth coat. She shut her eyes and leaned into my hand.

"Interesting. Mike could've forgotten."

I shrugged. "Possibly."

"You think something else is going on?"

Do I? "Maybe." I told her about the recliner.

Gina chuckled. "Even the Divas know that chair is sacred territory for you. He really said, 'No biggie?'"

"Yep."

"I bet he'd feel different if you took up residence in his favorite chair. Has anything happened to change the power structure in the relationship?" Gina asked.

I thought about the question. "Over breakfast, he asked about Brent. I told him about his moving to Seattle."

"Did you tell him about Peru and the proposal?"

"Yes. That may have been a mistake. It wasn't any of his business. I unintentionally blurted it out."

"So, he knows you said no, therefore his competition is gone. This should be interesting." Gina chuckled again. "You are about to see the true Mike Janson. Gotta go. Ciao!"

I crossed my ankles and scratched Buffy behind her silky curly ears. *The real Mike. Who is the real guy I've been dating all this time? I need more information.* I phoned Mike's home number, hoping to speak with Rachael.

She answered on the fifth ring, sounding winded.

"It's Phoenix. Is this a bad time?"

"No, I was taking a break after putting the baby down. Since I'd left my phone on the other side of the house, I had to run." She chuckled. "I can't seem to keep up with it and Aurora."

"How're things going?" I shifted to get more comfortable. Buffy gave me a baleful eye for disturbing her nap.

"It's been hard. I guess Dad told you about Mark." Her tone sounded wounded.

"Yes, I know how it feels to have an unfaithful husband." I was careful to not say, I know how you feel.

There was no response.

I wondered if we lost connectivity. "Rachael?"

"Your ex was unfaithful?"

"With three different women." The memory still bothered me.

"At the same time?" she asked, her tone incredulous.

"Yep."

"Wow. That's worse than Mark."

The remark didn't make me feel any better. It probably didn't make her feel better either. I turned on my side and pulled my knees up to ease my back.

Rachael made a conversational U-turn that threw me off track. "When will you know if Dad's test is negative, so you can come live with us? I could use the help. Dad suggested I could pump my breast milk. That way that you could take over some of the night-time feedings."

He did? I propped up on an elbow, my skin prickling. "What made you think I would move in with your Dad?"

"He told me. Said we'd ride out this coronavirus together. Do you have a dress yet for the wedding?"

My jaw dropped. "Wedding?"

"Dad called this morning and told me the way was clear, so y'all can get married in May."

A surge of anger and wayward hormones raced through my system. I felt like a human blowtorch ready to set fire to something. I rose onto my knees to turn on the ceiling fan. While the cool breeze helped to soothe my frustration, I had to unbutton the front of my shirt to release the heat spawned by my internal combustion.

I took a deep breath and tried to recover the purpose of my call. "Rachael, I don't know enough about your dad to move in, let alone get married."

"Oh! Sorry. Dad made it sound like it was a done deal."

Maybe in his mind, but not mine. "I need more information. Can you help me?"

"Well, sure. Dad's keen on marrying you."

"What was your mother like?"

Rachael paused before answering. "You remind me of her."

A chill crept down my spine, which helped to ease the hot flash. "In what way?"

"You look a lot like her. She was slender with long ginger hair."

"Really? Could you text me a photo of her?"

"Sure. Mom was a beauty. You can tell I look more like Dad. Give me a minute. I have one on my phone."

My hot flash subsided, so I buttoned my blouse and moved back to rest against the pillows. Buffy sneezed, shook herself, and jumped off the bed.

A text binged on my phone. I sat straight and opened it to find the photo from Rachael. Hunching over the phone, I enlarged it. My throat constricted while I stared at a woman who could've been my sister.

"Did you get it?" Rachael asked.

"Yes. Thanks." I cleared my throat. "What was your parents' marriage like? I'm asking, so I'll have a better idea of what to expect."

"Pretty traditional, I guess. Mom was the perfect little officer's wife," she said with a hint of sarcasm.

I chuckled. "Help me out here. I wasn't in the military, so what does that mean?"

"She kept the house clean and in order. She moved without complaint and adapted to the changes that Dad's career demanded. When Dad was away, Mom took over and ran everything with ease."

"And when he returned?" I asked.

"Things went back to Dad normal." More sarcasm.

I sat cross-legged. "What was, 'Dad normal?'"

"He was in charge, and Mom followed orders while waiting on him hand and foot. She told me Dad seduced her into marriage by rocking her world. Once they were married, the training began. He treated us like his personal troops. You may have noticed by now, Dad tends to get his way."

Fertile ground for thought. "If Mark asks for a divorce, do you plan to live with your Dad?" I asked.

"I wasn't so keen on the idea at first. I planned to keep the house and raise Aurora on my own."

"What changed your mind?"

"Dad insisted I should move in with y'all after you marry. He sold me on the idea of y'all helping to raise Aurora."

"I see." An ache began pounding my temples. I rubbed them, trying to ease the pain.

Rachael continued, "I was afraid I'd impinge on your privacy, but he said it wouldn't be a problem."

I felt like a pile of boulders had been dumped on me. It was time to claw my way out.

CHAPTER 36: More Information

After ending my call with Rachael, I texted the other Divas. *I need a Diva conference call tonight.*

No replies. Unlike me, they were all back at work.

I climbed off the bed, opened the door, and walked into the living room. Mike was on the sofa, his gaze glued to the television.

"I'm hungry. Want to help me make lunch?" I asked.

He glanced up. "Lunch would be great. Call me when it's ready."

Did he miss the 'help me' part? I walked over and turned off the TV.

His brows knitted into a scowl.

I smiled. "You can toast the bread while I get the ham, cheese, and condiments out."

His mouth dropped open. You'd have thought I asked him to run naked around the neighborhood.

Ignoring his lack of verbal response, I walked to the sink and washed my hands before going to the bread cabinet. I placed a partial loaf of wheat bread on the counter near the toaster.

Mike plodded toward the toaster.

Feeling a bit like his mother, I said, "Please wash your hands first."

He rinsed them.

"The plates are in the cabinet in front of you." I opened the fridge and brought out everything needed to make sandwiches.

He removed the plates and slammed the cabinet door.

I glanced at him. *He's acting like a passive-aggressive teenager.* After washing the tomato, I cut it into thick slices.

"The toast is ready," he mumbled.

Determined to be upbeat, I said, "Good. Let's make our sandwiches."

He waved me closer. "Let me show you how to make my sandwiches for the future."

He placed a mustard layer on the bottom slice of bread, followed by ham, cheese, lettuce, and tomato. He spread the top slice of toast with mayonnaise.

"Make sure you cut it on the diagonal." He smiled down at me with a patient look.

"I'll keep that in mind if you should ever become incapacitated."

He cocked his head. "What do you mean?"

"Unless you're ill, I'm not making your sandwiches. We can make them together."

His jaw dropped before he blurted, "Molly always made my sandwiches and brought them to me."

"I'm not your mother. Or your late wife."

We locked gazes.

He dropped his first.

Once we were seated, I said, "Tell me about Molly."

Looking uncomfortable, he delayed the answer by taking a bite and chewing. He swallowed and said, "Molly was great. Beautiful and funny, she anticipated my every need."

Leaning back in my chair, I cocked my head and said, "I called Rachael today."

He looked up from his plate and smiled. "That's nice. I'm glad you two get along."

"She seemed to be under the impression that if your COVID-19 test comes back negative, I'll be moving in until we get married. Where would she get such an idea?"

He gave me a sheepish look.

"She also informed me that we were marrying in May?"

He developed an intense interest in adjusting a lettuce leaf on his sandwich.

"Mike?"

"I, uh, thought since that Brent guy was moving to Seattle, there was no need to delay the wedding much longer."

My scalp tingled. "Did you ever think to ask me what I thought?"

He dropped his sandwich onto the plate. "You've been fiddle-farting around with this long enough, so I made a strategic decision. All we need is a few folks and a trip to the courthouse."

I crossed my arms before giving him *the look*. "First, weddings are planned by the bride, not the groom. Second, relationships aren't war games requiring strategic decisions. Third, you are not my commanding officer."

He wiped his hands on the napkin and slammed it down on the table. "I don't know why you're making this so damn hard. Molly would've been happy to go along with my plans."

I pulled my phone from my pocket and brought up Molly's photo. Placing it on the table, I turned it to face him.

His eyes widened. "Where did you..."

"I'm sure you notice the resemblance," I said.

His gaze dropped back to his sandwich.

My heart raced in my chest, remembering his reaction before I left for Peru. I tried to control the tremor in my voice. "I'm not Molly and never will be."

He shot me a hard look. "I know you're not Molly. You've certainly proved it today. I'm not stupid, you know."

I braced my hands on the table. "Never said you were." My mouth was dry as a stone. "Do you want to marry me because you want Molly back?"

Mike leaned forward. "You think I want you because of a resemblance to my deceased wife?"

"Unconsciously, yes," I said.

"Dammit to hell." He hammered the table with his fist.

I flinched. My pounding heartfelt ready to abandon my body and run.

He stood and leaned over the table. His menacing posture and steely glare reminded me of Jack Nicholson's before he yelled, "Son, you can't handle the truth," in the movie *A Few Good Men*.

I controlled my urge to run. Instead, I stood and faced him across the table. "Mike, I don't want to marry you so I can go into training to become your perfect wife, or get up in the middle of the night to feed your grandchild. I want an equal love relationship with the man I marry."

He straightened and ran both hands through his hair. "Come on, Phoenix, it's not like that, and you know it. Someone has to be in charge. I'm a man, so I'm the logical choice."

Silence dropped into place like a concrete wall.

"To hell with this!" He picked up his plate and slung it and the sandwich like a Frisbee across the kitchen. It hit a cabinet and shattered.

Our relationship shattered with it.

CHAPTER 37: What Now?

Too furious to appreciate the danger of the situation, I felt like Wonder Woman fueled by a super-sized, triple-shot latte.

"That's it!" I stood tall and pointed toward the door. My heart galloped inside my chest wall. "Get out. Now! I don't ever want to see or hear from you again."

His eyes widened with surprise at my reaction. He eased toward me with open arms. "My Darling Fish Lips, don't be this way. Sorry I broke your plate. I'll buy you another one if you want."

Pointing toward the door again, I said, "Out, or I'll call the police. I'm sure the officers will arrest you after they see the broken plate."

Holding his hands palm up, he smiled, bringing his dimples into play. "Come on, you wouldn't call the police over a little misunderstanding, would you?"

I picked up my phone and dialed 911. Keeping an eye on him, I said, "A man named Mike Janson is destroying property in my home, and he won't leave." I gave her my name and address. "Please hurry!"

"Do you feel you are in danger?" the operator asked.

"Yes."

Red-faced, Mike strode toward me, his gaze on my phone.

I shoved my chair between us, backed up, and yelled, "He's coming at me," before putting the call on speaker mode. Shifting to mirror his approach, I slipped the phone into my pocket and took a stance, the way my defensive arts teacher had taught me.

The operator said, "A car is in your vicinity and en route."

Mike halted, unsure how to proceed. He stomped to the other end of the house with clenched fists and disappeared into the guest room.

Dear God, don't let him have a gun.

Minutes later, he appeared with his satchel in hand, stepped into the bathroom, and raked his things into the bag before zipping it shut.

I reported with a trembling voice, "He's packing, but I'm not sure if he'll try something else."

The operator assured me a sheriff's deputy should be there in five minutes.

Five minutes!

Mike stopped in the living room and glowered. "You're nuts!" he yelled. "I can't believe you called the police because I threw a plate and broke it."

I hoped he'd yelled loud enough to be heard on the recording. *I'm nuts? I wasn't the one throwing a plate.*

Buffy ran through the dog door and stopped beside me. Sensing the tension, she emitted a low, menacing growl.

Mike pointed at her. "If that dog comes near me, I'll kick it into the next county."

I reached down and grabbed her collar. "If you touch my dog, it will be like the wrath of God descending on you."

He marched out, slamming the door behind him.

Buffy broke from my grasp and rushed to the door, snarling like a vicious pit bull.

I ran to the door and locked it.

"He left," I told the operator.

"Stay on the line until the officer arrives."

Two minutes later a deputy arrived, lights blazing.

***

Rachael called an hour later. She whispered into the phone, "What happened? Dad came home, cussing like an enlisted man, and went to his room. Isn't he still on quarantine?"

"Yes, he is, so stay away from him. I confronted him about the wedding, and then one thing led to another." I paused, feeling guilty. "I showed him your mother's photo and reminded him I wasn't Molly. I hope this doesn't cause a problem."

"Oh, shit. I'll catch blowback on this one," she said.

"Sorry. I didn't mean to make things hard for you."

"That's okay. You needed to know. Don't get me wrong, I'd love to have you join our family. You brought out the best in him."

"Did Mike ever intimidate your mom into doing things his way?"

"Off and on. Mom did her best to keep the peace."

"Did he ever throw things or attack her?"

"Not that I remember, but they were married three years before I came along. Why?"

I told her about the plate-throwing incident.

"Wow! You must have really defied him." She lowered her voice. "Gotta go. He's coming out of his lair."

Pacing, I prayed that Mike wouldn't take his anger out on Rachael and her baby.

My computer chirped the FaceTime tone.

I rushed to my office to answer with Buffy following, curious as usual. It was the Divas.

"Okay," Gina said. "We're all here. What's going on?"

I relayed the story, watching for each of their responses. Kat's lips thinned. Latishia had her neck thing going. To my amazement, Gina's curls appeared to grow in volume.

I rubbed the back of my stiff neck. "Heck, Mike probably passed the deputy on his way out of my neighborhood. The deputy took a report in case I have problems with him in the future."

Kat frowned, a line forming between her brows. "That's all you need—another Kent."

Kent was a guy I only dated twice, who turned into a stalker. When he followed the Divas to a restaurant one night, Kat recognized him and his voice. He was one of the first frat boys who raped her after someone slipped her a date-rape drug. Her son Jack was the outcome of that attack.

"I hope not. Mike was there when I threatened to shoot Kent if he didn't stop stalking me. I don't think Mike will forget that incident."

Gina looked ready to explode. "We never did give Mr. Kent his share of Diva justice."

"Karma will provide," Kat said. "If not, we can give it a little push after the pandemic ends."

"I'm in," said Latishia. "Where's Mike now? Wasn't he supposed to quarantine?"

"Home. Rachael phoned a few minutes ago to say he showed up in a bad mood and went to his room."

"Merita di essere schiacciato dai suoi testicoli."

"What?" Latishia asked. "Translate, Gina."

Gina huffed. "I said he deserves to have his testicles crushed. Who does he think he is, throwing plates in your house?" Her curls vibrated with each indignant move of her head.

Kat chimed in. "Throwing dishes is childish. I thought he was more mature."

"Yeah, he behaved like Todd," Latishia said. "Remember when the King of the Undertakers threw the coffee cup at Phoenix because she refused to pay half the legal fee for the divorce *he* wanted?"

"Don't remind me," I said, a shiver running over me. "At least Mike didn't aim the dish at me. He hit the kitchen cabinets."

Getting redder in the face, Gina asked, "Was it one of your grandmother's plates?"

"Yes. It was the set she collected way back when grocery stores offered tableware if you shopped with them."

"Mama talked about those dishes," Latishia said. "Each week, they offered a different part of the set, right?"

I nodded. "Lucky for me, Granny had a few extra pieces. I still hated to lose that plate."

Kat shook her head. "Sounds like Dr. Jekyll and Mr. Hyde. The minute Brent was out of the picture, Mike thought you were his, and the wall of niceness came down."

I shuddered at the memory of his angry expression. "Well, I went from two guys to no guys in a week. My problem dramatically resolved itself."

"Ain't that the truth." Latishia jutted her jaw forward. "Mama always said, 'Better an empty house than a bad tenant.'"

I nodded. "How true."

CHAPTER 38: Home Alone

I tried to sleep that night, but I couldn't. I tossed and turned, running through the events of the past two years—Dad's death from cancer, the divorce, and my dating fiascos after twenty years of marriage.

I reviewed my time with Brent and Mike. Brent and I might still be dating if not for his promotion and transfer. I cared for him like a dear friend, but I wasn't in love with him. I certainly didn't want his mom as a mother-in-law.

My relationship with Mike would take some time to autopsy. The day we met was fresh in my mind. The Divas were on vacation in Florida when I'd met Mike in the lobby of the hotel. My emergency room visit on our date that night had felt like life or death, bonding me to him.

Then there was the sex. Both men were attractive, sexy, and excellent lovers, but Mike and I had chemistry that my relationship with Brent lacked. More proof that it takes more than pheromones to make love work.

My mind whirled with information and comparisons. Full of frustration, I sat up and put on my robe. I trudged to the kitchen, where I made a cup of chamomile tea. Back in the living room, I found my DVD of *Mama Mia* and put it in the player. That movie may be the cure for many woes.

I settled down in the recliner, watched the film, and sipped the tea. It wasn't like I had to get up early for work, thanks to Mike. I had a day or two more of isolation until his test results came back.

***

I woke in the recliner with Buffy snuggled beside me. I yawned and stretched, letting the reality of the day settle on me like a freshly laundered sheet — a clean start.

I struggled out of the recliner, my partially numb limbs burning back to life. "Time for coffee, Buffy."

She gave a wide yawn, jumped to the floor, and shook.

It was quiet. I stood for a moment, relishing the stillness of the morning until Buffy's claws scraped the kitchen tile, disrupting the peace.

Typically, I rushed through the coffee-making process like an efficient android. Today, I inhaled the aroma of the grounds before starting the brew, making each step as Zen-like as possible. I poured the fragrant liquid into my mug, letting the steam caress my face. I took a sip after doctoring it. "Aaah!"

I slathered cream cheese on a toasted bagel while drawing in the wholesome aroma. The crunch of the bagel, mingling with the smooth cream cheese, was marvelous. I was content to sit at my breakfast table and watch the birds' antics at the feeder. Their different chirps of bird conversation cheered me.

It felt good to be still. On the trip to Peru, everything was fast-paced, cramming as much as possible into each day. When I'd planned the trip with the rest of the Divas, I'd had no idea of how it would change my life.

I compared it to our previous Florida trip. At the beach, each of us met a guy that would change our lives. Latishia and Aaron were talking about marriage. Kat continued to acclimate her Chinese parents to Don. Chris continued to steadily break down Gina's resistance to marriage.

I met Mike and rediscovered sex with him and Brent.

After each Diva trip together, we returned home to some form of crisis. When we returned to Alabama from the beach, we had barely had time to shelter in Latishia's basement when a tornado hit her neighborhood.

On the Peru trip, we arrived home in time for a pandemic. On top of that, I'd now lost both of the men who had played significant roles in my recovery from the divorce.

What a mess, and it isn't over yet.

Nothing had been the same since the trip to Peru. Yes, today things seemed more normal, yet different. I could intuit that my life would be permanently altered but wasn't sure exactly how.

I'd cleaned up breakfast and was changing the sheets when Rachael called.

"Do you have time to talk?" she asked, sounding near tears.

"Sure. Thanks to your Dad, I'm still in seclusion."

"Sorry about that." Her tone was sincere. "I'm worried about Dad."

I waited, choosing not to reply.

"He hasn't come out of his room."

I rolled my eyes, wondering if he'd manipulated her to call me. "Did he answer when you knocked?"

"He told me to go away."

"You do realize he is supposed to quarantine away from you and the baby. Make him a tray for breakfast, place it outside his door, and tell him it's there. Make sure he has a thermometer and bug him to take his temperature every hour."

"I'll try. What if Dad won't take the tray?"

"He's a man." I chuckled. "They seldom turn down food."

"If you say so." She didn't sound convinced when she ended the call.

I tapped my finger on the dresser. *What next?*

Kat's mindset possessed me. I cleaned and sanitized the entire house, which took two hours. Exhausted, I sat in my Lysol-treated recliner and eyed the clock. *What now?*

I balanced my checkbook, which killed another twenty minutes. The washer played the cheery tune that signaled the completion of the cycle. Desperate for anything to keep myself from thinking, I transferred the sheets to the dryer.

Buffy looked up at me, her tail twitching. *A walk. As long as I don't come close to anyone, it should be fine.*

I hooked my furry kid to a leash, grabbed my keys, and headed out the door. The day was glorious. My neighbor's honeysuckle scented the air, bringing back memories of sucking the sweet flowers as a child.

Buffy's tail wagged at maximum velocity while she tugged me down the driveway and onto the street. Like every walk with my dog, it was a sequence: A burst of speed followed by a quick stop to sniff mailboxes, fire hydrants, and blades of grass. I didn't care; I was happy to be out of the house. The sun warmed my face, and the flowers showed off their delicate beauty. *Spring, the sexiest time of the year, and I'm alone.*

Tears welled in my eyes. I swiped them away with my fingers. "Come on, Buffy. Time to go home."

I made it inside my house before the deluge of tears began. I unhooked Buffy and grabbed a box of tissues on my way to my recliner.

Buffy hopped up beside me and cuddled close. She could always read my moods. "I'll be okay, Sweetie. Heck, I'm not sure why I'm carrying on so."

Deep down, I knew. Grief.

Brent had been a good friend as well as a lover. Now he was gone. I'd probably never see him again. The memory of him dropping to his knee to propose brought a watery smile to my face. I allowed myself to feel the loss.

"Oh, shoot, I forgot to tell him I was negative for the virus."

I texted him. *Did you make it home from Peru?*

Yesterday. I must isolate for two weeks unless I can get tested.

Relief flooded me. *Glad you're home safe. FYI, our tests were negative.*

Good to hear. I'm packing. If all goes well, I plan to move in ten days.

Good luck. Stay safe.

He sent a thumbs up.

I didn't ask if he'd found a home or if his parents were still moving to Seattle. I wiped my tears and blew my nose before I fondled Buffy's curly ears. "You liked Brent, didn't you?"

She doggy smiled up at me like she understood.

I sniffled. "But you didn't care as much for Mike after he threw that plate, did you?"

She laid down and lowered her snout onto her paws.

I admit that I anthropomorphize my dog, but I swear she seems to know who is kind and who is a rascal. Can she tell by the way people smell?

A text binged on my phone.

"Probably Brent," I told Buffy, patting her head before picking up the phone.

Mike had texted, *Can we talk?*

"Calm down," I told myself. "Just because he texted, doesn't mean you have to reply right away or at all." I settled back into my chair and flipped on the television.

Several hours later, I wondered, *Is it hunger or anxiety that's gnawing my stomach?* While making a sandwich, I ran through my memory of the previous day. I started with my behavior. I wasn't proud of some of my antics. That completed, I analyzed Mike's assumptions, his passive-aggressive behaviors, the sandwich training episode, and his eventual meltdown.

I took my lunch to the table and munched while reviewing the events from a psychological perspective. If Rachael was correct, Mike demanded that his orders, expectations, and needs be met. It sounded like Molly had been worn down into a pattern of compliance to keep the peace. *Typical abuse patterns. She may not have viewed it that way, since many women only see being beaten half to death as abuse.*

Had I misinterpreted Mike's earlier amorous pursuit as wooing, rather than a persistent and calculated battle plan to win me as his territory?

I shoved chip after chip in my mouth, barely tasting them while I compared my memories to the new information I'd learned.

My conclusion? There were incidents of both typical courtship and stealthy manipulation. One point became as apparent as a clear mountain stream. After Brent was no longer a threat, Mike assumed he could have things his way. He'd won the war and had a right to the spoils. The sheer look of surprise and confusion on his face when I stood up to him after he treated my plate like a Frisbee provided valuable information. Like an out-of-control teenager, Mike was used to having his way. He had tried manipulation, temper tantrums, and intimidation to gain control and my compliance.

Some of his actions reminded me of the movie scenes where the drill sergeant broke down the troops and rebuilt them the military way. Sir, yes, Sir.

I'm not a saluting type of woman.

Another insight blossomed in my mind. Manipulation, temper tantrums, and intimidation were the same relationship tricks Todd had used to get his way.

I looked down at Buffy. "No way am I falling for that again!"

***

At seven that night, Rachael called. She sounded desperate. "Please talk to Daddy. He's in his room crying."

The angry woman in me wanted to hang up. The psychologist took over. I knew there was no way I would resume a relationship with Mike under any circumstance. What I didn't know was how far he would go to get me back.

I remembered a hospital consult where an alcoholic guy in his twenties swallowed a whole bottle of Tylenol. He thought it was a safe, fake suicide method to manipulate his battered, live-in girlfriend to come back home. It took him two hours to find her. Panicked, she called emergency services, and he was taken to the hospital. He told me, "It was just Tylenol! I only wanted to scare her into coming home." By then, the Tylenol had entered his bloodstream. The next day, the drug attacked his already damaged liver. He died a horrible death.

I focused back on the present. "Tell me more. Did Mike eat?"

She sniveled. "Yes, everything on the tray."

"That's a good sign. Does he show any signs of the virus?"

"Not that I know about. He said his temperature was normal."

The important question. "Did Mike state or indicate any suicidal intent?"

Rachael sucked in a breath. "No. He just keeps crying and telling me he blew it. He's really sorry. Can't you talk to him?"

I weighed my options. If I talked to Mike, it would make Rachael feel better. However, it would give him the impression the relationship wasn't over. He would try to wheedle his way back in through every form of manipulation he could devise. No way was I willing to become an emotional hostage. Besides, it would give him false hope and extend his emotional pain.

"My recommendation is to keep a close eye on him. If he threatens suicide, call 911. Make sure he has no pills, especially Tylenol, in his room. Remove any guns and sharp objects from the house. He may not be suicidal, but it'll make you feel better."

"Oh, my gosh." She sounded scared.

"I'm not trying to frighten you, but men who are used to having their way may try extreme measures and accidentally hurt themselves."

"I hadn't thought of that."

Silence filled the airways.

She blurted, "I can't handle this. I have a baby to see after. I don't see why you won't talk to him? Don't you care that he's suffering?"

One of my favorite sayings skittered into my mind and right out my mouth. "Pain is inevitable: suffering is optional."

Sounding more frustrated, Rachael asked. "What the hell does that mean?"

"Sorry. I was thinking out loud. It means it's normal and healthy for your dad to feel the grief of losing a relationship. It's his choice as to how he handles it, and how much he suffers." I cleared my throat. "You need to understand, and Mike needs to accept, I have no intention of resuming a relationship with him. To talk with him would only prolong his pain because it would encourage him to hold on. He needs to let go and feel the loss, so he can move forward."

Rachael hung up on me.

CHAPTER 39: One Last Attempt

The next morning, I was finishing my second cup of coffee when my doorbell rang.

A thrill of danger slithered over me. "Mike?"

Buffy ran toward the door, barking like a vicious attack dog.

Grabbing my phone, I rushed to the door and peeked through the peephole.

A guy in his twenties held a large arrangement of red roses in a glass vase.

I put Buffy in the bedroom and donned a mask before opening the door.

"Are you Phoenix O'Leary?"

"That's me."

He thrust the flowers at me. The delicate fragrance wafted around me.

I held up my hands and took a step back. "Would you hold them while I read the card?"

He grinned. "Sure."

I unpinned it from the red ribbon and opened the tiny envelope. *I love you! Please forgive me and give me a second chance.*

I paused, giving my racing heart a chance to steady. Not good. A no-win situation. *If I keep them, he'll move on to the next manipulation. If I refuse them, I look like an ungrateful bitch.*

"I can't accept these roses."

The guy lowered the arrangement. "What am I supposed to do with them?"

"Would you give me a moment?"

He nodded.

I hurried to my office and brought my computer back to life. I typed, *Our relationship is over. Accept this and move on. Rerouting the flowers to your home. I'm sure Rachael will enjoy them. Respect my wish to stop all contact. Phoenix*

I didn't handwrite or sign the note, to indicate emotional distance. I printed the page and placed it in an envelope with his full name on the front.

On a separate sheet, I wrote Mike's address down. I stopped by my purse and pulled out ten bucks.

I handed the man the letter and address. "Deliver the roses to this address, tell whoever answers that I refused the order, and give him or her this envelope."

He took them. If his downturned mouth was any indication, he was annoyed.

I handed him the tip. "Sorry for the inconvenience."

His countenance brightened. "No problem. Thanks."

He started to turn and stopped. "He must have messed up bad for you to refuse two dozen roses."

I nodded and closed the door.

***

After dinner, I texted the Divas. *FaceTime*.

I answered the call on my computer. Pleased to see their faces, I asked, "How's it going, ladies?"

Kat grinned. "I have good news. Dr. Howard asked me to call and tell you Mike's test came back negative."

I whooped. "I'm free!"

"I have some interesting news." Latishia grinned. "Phoenix, do you remember Brandi with an 'i'?"

Heat flushed my face. "Are you referring to the slut who had an affair with Todd while he was married to me?"

"The very one. Girl, she got fired today for embezzling money."

"You're kidding." While I didn't think much of the squeaky-voiced blonde, I hadn't expected this.

"Nope." Her eyes twinkled. "It gets better. The police showed up and handcuffed her at her desk. Hauled her out the door and put her in the back of a police car."

Gina, who was using her phone for the call, asked, "How is everyone reacting at the bank?" I felt a little dizzy because she was walking, which shifted the image around.

"If you don't stand still, I might get sick," Kat said, holding her hand over her mouth.

Gina sat. "Sorry."

Latishia said, "The bigwigs are closed-mouthed about it. The rest are gossiping like crazy, but no one knows how or why she did it."

"I wonder how long it's been happening?" *I wonder if Todd is involved.*

Latishia shrugged. "Who knows?"

"Things have been slow on my end. The rising COVID-19 cases are biting into my business," Gina said.

"This is only the beginning. Dr. Howard interned at Mount Sinai Hospital in New York City, so he has contacts up there. This is going to be a major ordeal. Go to the stores and pull in supplies for at least six weeks. Think canned and frozen goods, paper products, and cleaning products. Prepare to isolate for up to six weeks."

"You're kidding!" Gina said.

"No, I'm not. Doc told me he started preparing for this while we were on vacation. I suggest we meet for dinner tomorrow night for an early celebration of Gina's birthday. It may be the last time we get together for a while. They'll close the restaurants day after tomorrow, except for take-out."

Gina grinned. "I vote Cantina Laredo at Bridge Street, since I'm the birthday girl."

"Sounds good to me. I could use a margarita." I said.

Gina asked, "Phoenix, what's the latest on Mike?"

I told them about the roses and my response.

"Girl, you should've sent those roses my way. I could use a little glamour in my life."

I chuckled. "How would you explain red roses to Aaron?"

Latishia leaned closer to the screen and winked. "I'd think of something."

Kat frowned. "Two dozen red roses is a serious make-up bouquet."

"I'm sure Rachael is enjoying them." I updated them on her latest phone call.

"Goodness, does she think you're her private therapist?" Gina asked.

I shrugged and pulled Buffy into my lap. "I hope she doesn't call again."

Gina almost bounced in her seat. "Mom and Dad bought me a puppy for my birthday."

Latishia clapped. "Do you have it now?"

"I get her Friday night."

"What kind of dog is she?" I asked while scratching Buffy.

"A Yorkie." She looked at her watch. "It's getting late. Drat, I haven't bought dog supplies and groceries yet."

We signed off. I hugged Buffy. "You're about to have a doggie cousin."

CHAPTER 40: Preparing for the Worst

The next morning, I rose with a purpose. I dressed, ate breakfast, and skipped the second cup of coffee. My mission was to prepare for a pandemic.

The freedom of driving down the street was lovely. Trees and flowers showed off their blooms. Sunshine bounced off the windshield, forcing me to put on my shades.

The first stop was Home Depot. I put on my mask before exiting the car. Once inside, I strode straight to the appliance section, where I spotted the small chest freezer I'd been considering for some time. Within forty minutes, I'd made the purchase. Thanks to a last-minute cancellation, the clerk assured me the delivery man could install it that afternoon.

Feeling pleased with my progress, I drove across the parking lot to Costco. I filled my gas tank and found a parking spot close to the door of the building. Dad used to say it was spooky the way one always opened for me.

Channeling Kat, I pulled out a sanitary wipe and cleaned the cart like a real nurse practitioner. My first stop was paper goods, where I wrangled giant packages of toilet paper, paper towels, napkins, and tissues into my cart. Feeling a bit winded, I leaned against a display and checked my list. I rolled over to the wine section and chose three bottles each of my favorites. Feeling good about my progress, I collected the rest of the items that didn't require refrigeration. I managed to nab the last three-pack of Lysol spray and two containers of Clorox wipes. I saved the meat department for last, grabbing two three-packs each of organic ground beef, chicken, and bison. I checked my list and doubled back for eggs and a large bag of dog food.

My cart was so full I couldn't see over the top of the merchandise. A long wait in line tested my patience. Once I checked out, I loaded my Prius to the roof and drove home. I felt pretty good about my day so far, but I knew I wasn't finished.

After consulting by phone with Latishia, Kat, and Gina's mom, I petted Buffy's head and drove to Wal-Mart. My first stop was the pet department. The Divas had all decided to give Gina pet supplies for her new puppy as birthday gifts. Mine would be a new collar, leash, and harness. I found the dog section and nearly panicked. Everything looked too large for a Yorkie puppy. After several minutes of searching, I found a few pieces on the end of the aisle that were the right size. I chose a pink matching set.

Feeling high from my success, I headed to the grocery section. Shelves were almost empty on the canned goods and paper product aisles. People rushed past me with panicked expressions and carts piled high with groceries. I loaded a month's worth of stuff into my cart, including a few naughty snacks that should've stayed on the shelf.

Another long line. The lady in the queue next to mine hungrily eyed my link sausages. I suspected if I turned my back, she'd sneak them out of my cart. Grocery shopping has never been my favorite activity, but the atmosphere today was oppressive. Even worse, people were staring at my mask like I was a space alien.

I ran a list through my mind, wondering if I'd forgotten anything, while driving home. With the sun shining, it was hard for me to imagine a virus I couldn't see was killing humans across the globe.

I'd barely had time to unload and put away my items when a truck backed into my drive.

A lanky man in his thirties jumped down from the compartment with a clipboard. "You Phoenix O'Leary?"

"That's me."

A younger tousle-headed man stepped out of the passenger side and ran his hands through his hair.

"Where do you want this freezer?" The lanky man asked.

I signaled for him to follow and showed him where to install the new chest freezer.

"Good, there's a 120-volt grounded plug here. You won't have to call an electrician."

Within twenty minutes, they had my new freezer installed and were on their way to their next delivery.

I decided to keep all the frozen items in my fridge overnight, so the new appliance could reach the appropriate frigid temperature.

My Apple watch vibrated to alert me that Governor Kay Ivey would hold a press conference about the coronavirus. I headed to my chair and remoted on the TV.

I stared at the screen in disbelief. In two days, a shelter in place order would occur. "Good grief! I'm finally out of quarantine and now I have to shelter in place!" I said to no one.

Thirty minutes later, I was still considering what this would mean for my next three weeks when my answering service phoned.

"Dr. O'Leary, have you heard about the shelter in place order?" Jane asked.

"Yes. I was about to call and discuss it with you. I suppose we should call and cancel more appointments."

"Your patients have been calling in droves to cancel their sessions. The bad news is your schedule is clear for the next four weeks."

I gulped a deep breath to steady myself.

"The good news is you have a full schedule for the two weeks after," Jane said, sounding chipper.

I sighed with resignation. "It is what it is. We'll handle emergency calls as usual. Please tell the staff to stay safe and well."

Buffy padded into the room, and doggy grinned up at me.

"Looks like it's going to be us girls." I clapped, and Buffy joined me in the chair. "Let's catch a few winks before Gina's birthday dinner."

CHAPTER 41: Happy Birthday!

It feels different going to a restaurant for a meal, when you know the next day, only take out will be available. Thinking back to my days of working in an alcohol and drug facility, I could relate to the addicts' 'party hardy' philosophy before entering treatment.

Bridge Street Towne Center was busy, so finding a parking space was difficult. When I arrived, the Divas stood clustered beside the door to the restaurant.

Kat waved me forward. "Good, I asked for a table in the back, far from everyone. We're treating this like we did airplanes. Sanitize, sanitize, sanitize."

I saluted. "Yes, ma'am."

Kat arched a brow at me. "Mess with me, and I'll Lysol you."

"Too late, Latishia already did that the day y'all left my house."

We burst into laughter.

Kat used a wipe to open the door. We followed the hostess to our table and cleaned everything we might touch before piling all of Gina's presents on the far end of the table.

A young man, followed by our waitress, brought chips and dip to the table.

I squinted at her name tag. "Carlita, today is our friend's birthday." I gestured toward Gina.

"Happy Birthday," Carlita said, with a face-spitting grin.

"We need two top-shelf guacamoles. Please put them on my bill." She nodded. "Anything to drink?"

"Four margaritas," said Latishia. "I'm covering those."

Kat raised a finger to catch Carlita's attention. "Please bring us four glasses of water, too."

"I'll be back with your drinks and guac."

I turned to Kat. "What do you think about the Governor's shelter in place order?"

She pushed her glasses back in place. "I think it's too late. It should've been ordered two weeks ago. We shouldn't be out tonight, but I hated to not celebrate Gina's birthday."

"Family court is closing, so I'll be working from home," Gina reached for a chip. "I can conference call my clients if necessary."

Latishia dipped her chip into the salsa. "I'll start working from home on Monday. It looks like I'm stuck homeschooling Dante while trying to work."

Gina grimaced. "That doesn't sound like much fun. Better you than me." She popped her dry chip into her mouth and crunched down.

Kat looked worried. "I'm considered essential personnel, so I have to work. That leaves homeschooling to my parents."

I unwrapped the flatware and placed my napkin in my lap. "Bless their little hearts." *Trying to teach a socially isolated, bored teenager doesn't sound like fun to me.*

Kat patted my arm. "On the bright side, I'm happy Mike is out of your house."

"Me, too. It was getting freaky."

Carlita returned, balancing a tray with four glasses of ice water. None too soon for me since I'd swallowed a salsa-laden chip. The moment she placed mine on the table, I gulped down a third of the glass.

I rasped, "That's hotter than usual." My lips and the inside of my mouth burned.

Latishia burst into a hearty laugh, then stopped. Her mouth formed an O. "Gotta go!"

She shot from her seat and walked with her thighs close together toward the ladies' room.

Gina tracked her progress, then turned to face us. "Hope she's wearing an emergency pad." She turned toward Kat, who was to her right. "She has more problems in that area than the rest of us. Why?"

"Women who are heavier and have had children tend to experience more bladder drop," Kat said.

"Here she comes," I whispered.

Latishia eased into her chair. "Phew, that was close. Oh, good. Here comes the guacamole. I'm famished. Stress makes me hungry."

Carlita carried a tray stand. A waiter followed her, holding a large round tray above his head. She positioned the stand before the guy settled the tray with the fixings on top of it.

Her brown eyes twinkled. "Thanks, Joe."

While we watched, she scraped out the flesh from fresh avocadoes into two bowls and mashed it with a fork. She deftly added lime, fresh cilantro, garlic, pico de gallo, and diced jalapenos. She mixed it all together and cleaned the edges of the bowls with the limes.

Placing both bowls on the table, she tilted her head and said, "I'll be right back with your drinks," and took away the tray and stand.

True to her word, she came back within minutes with our margaritas.

I sipped mine with closed eyes, knowing it might be a long time before I returned. *Wonderful.*

I put the drink down and picked up my menu. "We best decide on an entrée."

After a quick glance, Latishia put down her menu. "I'll have the chicken fajitas." She held up a hand. "I know I should try something else, but I love the dish."

Kat peeked over the top of her menu. "I'm having the Espinaca."

Latishia cocked her head. "What's that?"

Kat read, "'Two enchiladas with sautéed spinach, Monterey Jack, and mushrooms, with sour cream poblano sauce.' Sounds yummy."

Gina closed the menu. "I'm having the chicken chimichanga. I love burritos."

Everyone looked at me. "It's hard to decide because everything I've eaten here is wonderful." My gaze skimmed back and forth over the menu. "I'm going with the Veracruz."

Gina picked up her menu and scanned it. "Here it is, 'two pulled chicken, spinach and Monterey jack enchiladas with tomatillo sauce, marinated vegetables, and queso fresco.'" She looked up. "That's similar to Kat's dish, only with chicken."

Carlita joined us. "Has everyone decided?"

We gave our dinner orders and waited until she left before resuming our conversation.

Latishia scowled when her thin chip broke off into the guac. She used her spoon to fish the chip to the side of the bowl.

"You might use the spoon to scoop it onto the chip," I suggested. "I love their thin crispy chips, but they don't hold up to scooping guac."

We focused on our dips and drinks. With each bite and sip, I felt my underlying anxiety about the current state of the world easing.

Kat dabbed at her mouth with her napkin leaving lipstick on the white cloth. "How do y'all plan to shelter in place over the next two to four weeks?"

I mumbled around a mouthful, "It won't be with Mike, that's for sure."

Latishia wiped her hands. "Aaron is moving in tomorrow. We all discussed it and decided we didn't want to be separated. He'll work from the spare bedroom. Daddy's shop is considered an essential service, so it will stay open. He may have to reduce hours for some of his guys." She spread her napkin in her lap. "Kat, he wants to talk to you about how to keep his staff safe."

Kat nodded. "I'll call him tomorrow."

"What about Mama Snide's catering service?" I asked.

She provided soul-food lunches to several local engineering firms.

"Mama has temporarily lost her catering contracts. Her customers are furloughing their staff, or they're working from home," Latishia said.

Looking alarmed, Gina said, "What's she going to do?"

"Mama's only working because she loves it so much. She gets Social Security, and her only monthly bills are for food costs. She'll be fine." Latishia sipped her drink. "I think she plans to go cook with the Meals on Wheels folks at the Senior Center."

A line of concern formed between Kat's brows. "Mama Snide and Willy are in the high-risk category. In fact, that applies to both Gina's and my parents. I'll also be talking to all of them about safety."

Latishia looked worried. "I hadn't thought about that."

"Gina, who are you and your new puppy sheltering with during the big shutdown?" I asked.

"I could go to Mom and Dad's house, but I'm not sure I would live through it. I guess it will be just Phoebe and me." She didn't look happy about the situation.

Gina's a social person who enjoys working around people. She often has eaten dinner out to avoid too much time alone.

I grinned. "Your Yorkie's name is Phoebe? How cute."

Gina pulled out her phone, swiped until she found the pup's photo, and passed it around. We oohed and aahed over the furry face with black button eyes.

"I'll pick her up after dinner. I plan to stop by Wal-Mart to stock up with what she needs. She'll fit right into my purse."

Latishia harrumphed. "You'll have to take out the kitchen sink before you squeeze the little darlin' inside."

Gina gave her a fake glare. "Some friend. Picking on me during my birthday dinner."

Wanting to waylay one of their recreational baiting sessions, I answered Kat's earlier question. "It'll be Buffy and me—all alone."

Since the divorce adjustment phase, I've enjoyed living alone, but like Gina, I socialize a good bit and will miss it.

"Phoenix, you can visit us," Latishia said.

Kat threw up her hands. "No visiting. Not even with your parents, unless you drop off groceries and leave them at the door."

"Anthony lives with my parents. He can do the grocery runs," Gina said.

Carlita arrived with our entrees and placed them in front of us.

Mine was delicious. If the moans of appreciation heard from the others were any indication, theirs were, too.

Twenty minutes later, I scraped the last of the cheese sauce off my plate, ate it, and sighed with contentment.

A chorus of Happy Birthday caught everyone by surprise, except Kat, who looked pleased.

Carlita placed a sizzling Mexican apple pie with a burning candle in front of Gina.

She blew it out and grinned.

Carlita added a giant sizzling chocolate walnut brownie with ice cream.

"Happy birthday." Carlita pointed at the apple pie plate. "That is cinnamon ice cream."

"Yum!" Kat rubbed her hands together. She looked at the waitress. "Remember, the dessert goes on my tab."

Carlita nodded. "I'll be right back with small plates and spoons so y'all can share."

Usually a chocolate lady, I surprised myself by liking the apple dessert better.

When we finished, I wasn't sure we'd be able to rise from the chairs until the next morning.

"Time for presents," Kat announced. "This one is from me."

Gina ripped the paper off a large box and opened it with her table knife. Out came a pink, poufy dog bed, the correct size for a Yorkie, along with a bag of puppy food.

She hugged the bed to herself. "It's perfect."

I stood and handed her mine.

When Gina pulled out the collar, harness, and leash, tears welled in her eyes. "These are the ones I planned to buy. Thank you."

"Me next." Latishia handed her a huge box.

Gina had to stand to reach around it. When she managed to open it, she pulled out a pet crate and two bowls with a Yorkie photo on the bottom. She passed around the dishes for inspection.

I laughed as I examined the design. "Adorable. This is more like a puppy shower than a birthday party."

I glanced at the end of the table, where three cardboard boxes still sat. "What's in those boxes?"

Kat stood and gave one apiece to Latishia, Gina, and me. "Inside, you'll find a dozen N-95 protective masks and a box of gloves. There are instructions for how to use them to protect yourselves from COVID-19. Utilize them correctly, and don't waste them. I suspect they may become scarce."

I held my box like it contained precious jewels. "Can you spare these?"

She nodded. "Dr. Howard is a forward thinker. He stockpiled extra supplies back when the CDC was concerned about the Bird Flu."

We all thanked her and asked her to express our gratitude to Dr. Howard.

Gina, Latishia, and I ordered Mexican decaf coffee that smelled like cinnamon. Kat asked for a cup of hot water and pulled a chamomile tea bag from her purse.

Latishia's lower lip protruded. "How're we gonna see each other with this stay at home order?"

"FaceTime," I suggested.

Gina sighed before taking a sip from her cup. "It's better than nothing."

Kat raised her cup. "We'll always have Peru."

We clinked the brims and said, "Peru."

I wrapped my hands around my cup to absorb the warmth. "What's your favorite memory about Peru?"

Latishia grinned. "Aranwa Hotel in Sacred Valley. I could spend a week there looking at the plants and trees. Being surrounded by the lush vegetation and the running water relaxed me. I didn't realize how kinked I was until I arrived there and was able to relax."

Gina stretched and yawned. "Who wouldn't be yanked in a knot after the journey to get there. I thought the marathon through Miami's airport would do me in before I ever made it to South America."

Giggling, Kat said, "We could make it an annual event and call it the suitcase dash."

"Heck, why not make it the Airport Olympics," I said, holding my arms wide. "We could introduce the new sport of luggage tossing. Baggage handlers from all over the world could compete."

Gina waved her hands like when she's trying to remember a word. "The find your gate maze. It could be a timed event."

We chatted for a while about our individual takes on the airport experience.

"The air travel wasn't my favorite part, but Machu Picchu made up for the trauma." I shifted in my seat and finished off my coffee. "I'm happy I saw the site while I could still hike it." I winced. "Those high rock steps turned the muscles in my legs into concrete for days."

"Despite all the eating, I lost ten pounds on that trip," Gina said.

Kat leaned on the table. "I loved the area where they dug those circle terraces into the ground and experimented with the crops. Jack's doing a paper on that for school. What was the name of the place?"

"Moray," I said. "I also enjoyed the train ride. In fact, most of Peru was beautiful, but I wouldn't want to live there."

Kat shook her head. "I'm relieved we didn't get stuck there. It was a close call."

Gina looked at her watch and jumped up. "I need to get going. My folks are waiting to give me Phoebe."

We paid our bills and helped Gina to her car with her presents. After loading them into her trunk, we embraced like we might never hug again.

CHAPTER 42: Sheltering at Home

I'd been alone with Buffy for a week. She followed me everywhere. I missed my lunches out and dinners with the Divas. Heck, I missed interacting with my clients.

So far, I'd cleaned the house, tried on my clothes to determine what to donate to charity, and organized my closets. Discards were piling up in the garage. I'd averaged a movie a day and found myself addicted to *The Great Pottery Throw Down* on YouTube. This wouldn't be so strange if I'd ever thrown a pot. My FaceTime calls with the Divas helped.

A call from my office manager surprised me.

"Mrs. Jones wants to know if she can continue her sessions on Skype."

I thought a moment. "How would we work out payments?"

Nancy said, "I can schedule the appointment and let them pay by credit card. I'll text you and post it on your calendar as usual with a phone number to call."

"Let's do it. Isolation isn't good for mental health problems." I said.

I knew this wasn't going to be like a normal week in my practice, but it would be good to provide some level of help.

I'd never been lonely before, but today I felt that way. Too much time alone with too little to keep me occupied. I'd decided to clean out all my drawers when the doorbell rang.

Buffy took off like a shot, barking with vigor.

Mike? I shuddered with dread.

I peeked out the door and saw a fuzzy face with black eyes. Rearing back, I looked again.

I flung open the door and there stood Gina and Phoebe.

Gina looked desperate. "Can we shelter at home together? I can't do this alone."

I opened my arms and hugged her. "Come on in. Where's your stuff?"

"In my trunk."

She placed Phoebe on the floor. Buffy and the puppy that was half her size walked in circles, sniffing each other's backsides.

Gina crossed her arms and cocked her head in my direction. "I love you like a sister, Phe, but we're not doing that."

We both laughed.

"Pull into the garage," I said.

We spent the rest of the day unloading Gina's car, setting up Phoebe, and moving Gina into the guest room.

That night after dinner, we held a video conference call with Latishia and Kat to tell them Gina and Phoebe would be staying at my house for the lockdown.

"You learn a whole lot about a man when you're isolated with him for a week." Latishia said. She leaned closer and lowered her voice. "The man farts like a horse when he eats chili."

When we stopped laughing, Kat wiped her eyes and said, "I needed a good laugh. We've been really busy at Doc's office. It's so stressful and uncomfortable wearing PPE all the time." She touched her cheeks. "I think I'm developing a mask rash."

"I'm grateful you're not working in the emergency room," I said.

"Amen!" Latishia said. "Did you decide what to do with your practice, Phoenix?"

"I've closed the office to patients, but I am doing a few video sessions. I won't see as many clients during a week, but I'll be able to help the ones who need it most."

Gina poked me. "I'm sure it's not the same as a face to face session. You can't even hand them a tissue."

I shrugged. "It is what it is. I've lost both men in my life, I'm isolating with a friend and my new doggie niece, and I'm doing video therapy. Things could be much worse."

THE END

Photos from Peru

Machu Picchu

Cusco, Peru

Moray (Inca ruin)

Native girl in Square at Cusco

San Francisco Monastery in Lima, Peru

Made in the USA
Monee, IL
14 April 2025

15743658R00125